MORE PRAISE FOR "A WAIST IS A TERRIBLE THING TO MIND"

"*A Waist is a Terrible Thing to Mind* is a wake-up call for us all. It poignantly documents the insidious and negative influence the diet and fashion industries exert on women's self-esteem. The book challenges all of us, men and women, to redefine beauty in a way that will promote self-acceptance and wellness. Let us accept the challenge!"

Mimi Guarneri, M.D • Cardiologist
Medical Director, Scripps Center for Integrative Medicine

•

"This book exposes our cultural obsession with weight and the misogynistic toll it takes on women with a unique, heartfelt and articulate collection of personal stories. The compelling women's voices on these pages expose our pervasive, ubiquitous psychic abuse around being thin, with an immediacy and urgency that we all need to understand. This is an important and necessary read."

Belleruth Naparstek
author, Your Sixth Sense
creator of The Health Journeys *guided imagery audio series*

•

"A revelatory treasure of human experiences, opening the reader's eyes to the torments imposed by the mindless worship of pop images of beauty."

Erving Polster Ph.D. • Miriam Polster, Ph.D.
authors • Co-Directors, Gestalt Training Center, San Diego, California

•

"This outstanding book gives a voice to countless women's struggles with body image, revealing the magnitude of this crisis. These stories cannot be read without affecting the readers. This book challenges women to reclaim their bodies and create their own healthy, attainable beauty ideals."

Ann Kearney-Cooke, Ph.D.
Director, Cincinnati Psychotherapy Institute
Scholar, Partnership for Women's Health, Columbia University, New York

•

"This book is a gold mine. As one who has always been awed by the marvelous complexity of the human body since I first began my medical training, I feel despair in the recognition that so many women are so unhappy with their miraculous bodies. Yet I also feel hope that this book will begin to change what has become a very real problem for over half of our population. Reading this book is something we all owe ourselves."

Lana Holstein, MD.
author • Director of Women's Health, Canyon Ranch

A WAIST IS A TERRIBLE THING TO MIND

JAN PHILLIPS
CATHY CONHEIM
CHRISTINE FORESTER

AND A CIRCLE
OF WOMEN

Breakthrough Press • P. O.Box 135 • La Jolla • California 92038

Copyright © 2000 by Jan Phillips, Cathy Conheim, LCSW, and Christine Forester

Published by Breakthrough Press
P. O.Box 135 • La Jolla • California 92038
Fax: 858. 454-5959
e-mail: info@breakthroughpress.com
website: www.breakthroughpress.com

Co-authors:
Jan Phillips • Cathy Conheim • Christine Forester • and a Circle of Women

Editor:
Jan Phillips

Cover design, book design and illustrations:
Christine Forester Catalyst

A Cover Story—or The Story of a Cover © 2000 Christine Forester, reproduced here
with the author's permission.

Library of Congress Cataloging-in-Publication Data
Phillips, Jan
Conheim, Cathy
Forester, Christine
     A Waist is a Terrible Thing to Mind
     ISBN 0-9679576-0-5

     1. Self-help   2. Psychology   3. Women's studies   4. Eating disorders
     1. Title

What is this self inside us, this silent observer,
Severe and speechless critic, who can terrorize us
And urge us on to futile activity,
And in the end, judge us still more severely
For the errors into which his own reproaches drove us?

• T. S. Eliot •
The Elder Statesman

Art begets art. When Cathy Conheim, a psychotherapist, and two Ob-Gyns, Donna Brooks, M.D. and Barbara Levy, M.D., commissioned the Real Women sculptures as a way of using art to initiate a new dialogue about body image and women's health, little did they know what they were starting.

When a poet first encountered the sculptures of thirteen women's bodies, she was inspired to write a poem to each woman which is now an essential part of the Real Women Project. When a singer-songwriter saw the sculptures and read the poems, she was inspired to write a song that has since touched the lives of thousands of people. When a video producer listened to the music, saw the sculptures and read the poems, she created a video revealing the beauty and elegance of women from around the world.

When women around the country visited the Real Women website and were asked to tell their own stories, hundreds did. Many revealed histories of shame and abuse, struggles and sorrow, hollow victories and full-bodied failures in their battles against a beauty narrowly-defined. One story after another contributed to a bigger story, an epic tale of a culture's obsession with beauty and the destruction left in its wake.

This book is an alarming and dramatic exposé of the profound impact of body image on women's lives. It is a record of real losses incurred by real women who have spent lifetimes in pursuit of an artificial beauty—a beauty defined by profiteers that is neither attainable nor authentic. It will not bring down the $40 billion diet industry that thrives on women's vulnerability, but it may build up women's resistance to its insidious message that we are not acceptable exactly as we are.

Lives are lost each year as beautiful, healthy young women starve themselves to death. Millions of us are suffering depression and anxiety as the media pellets us with starvation imagery and empty promises. We are struggling for our lives here, for the lives of our children, and our stories are our only weapons.

Many of our stories are difficult to share, painful to read, but bringing them to light is the first step toward healing. We cannot change what we do not understand, and we cannot understand what we have not articulated. It is our stories that reveal us to ourselves and others, remind us that we're not alone, shed a light on what we must change in order to grow. We must start with what *is* before we move on to what *can be*.

It is our hope that as art inspires art, these stories will inspire women to come together and tell their own, for it is in these circles of trust that healing begins.

ACKNOWLEDGEMENTS

In the early stages of this book, we had only the contributions of women who had found their way to the Real Women Project web site and shared their pains and tribulations there. Their stories were so compelling that we issued a call for submissions, hoping to generate more stories and circles of women communicating on the subject. Notices were sent to members of the International Women's Writing Guild, who in turn sent word out to their writing circles, and so it rippled.

Although there was no compensation for their time, no promise of publication, women from every part of the country sent in their stories, contributing to this new dialogue about body image and beauty.

It was not an easy decision to opt for anonymity through the use of first names only, when the writers are certainly deserving of credit. Many contributors to this book requested use of their first names only, so we chose that as our style for the sake of consistency. We realize that these individuals, in their anonymity, speak for thousands who might not write but need to be heard.

We also posted an invitation for stories on the Ms. Magazine website. The ensuing cyber-conversation is included with only minor edits.

The stories we received led us down roads none of us had expected to travel. We compiled *A Waist is a Terrible Thing to Mind* as a collective acknowledgement of women's experience, a call to self-awareness, and a call to action. We are deeply grateful to the writers who shared their stories generously and courageously. We hope that this work contributes to a better world, a more tolerant and healing environment for those to come.

So may it be.

TABLE OF CONTENTS

ALARMING FACTS

- The average American woman is 5'-4", weighs 140 pounds and wears a size 14 dress. The "ideal" woman portrayed by models, Miss America, Barbie dolls, and screen actresses is 5'-7", weighs 100 pounds and wears a size 8.

- 1/3 of all Americas wear a size 16 or larger.

- 75% of American women are dissatisfied with their appearance; 50% of American women are on a diet at any one time.

- Between 90 and 95% of reducing diets fail to produce long-term weight loss.

- A full 2/3 of dieters regain the weight within one year, virtually all regain it within five years.

- The diet industry, which includes diet foods, diet programs and diet drugs, takes in over $40 billion each year and is still growing; quick weight-loss schemes are among the most common consumer frauds, and diet programs have the highest customer dissatisfaction of any service industry.

- Young girls are more afraid of becoming fat than they are of nuclear war, cancer, or losing their parents.

- 50% of 9-year-old girls and 80% of 10-years-old girls have dieted; 90% of junior and senior high school female students diet regularly, even though only between ten and fifteen percent are over the weight recommended by the standard weight charts.

- 1% of teenage girls and 5% of college-age women become anorexic or bulimic.

- Most bulimics report that the onset of their disorder occurred while they were dieting.*

- Anorexia has the highest mortality rate, up to 20 %, of any psychiatric diagnosis. Girls develop eating and self-image problems before drug or alcohol problems. There are drug and alcohol programs in almost every school but no eating disorder programs.

Excerpts from 1996 Council on Size and Weight Discrimination for Mount Mary, New York.
* *Full Voice*, published by The Body Shop.

1

A Cover Story — or the Story of a Cover

Tick.Tock.Tick.Tock.

Grandfather clock.
Predictable.
Dependable.
Comforting Tick,Tock.
Chiming,
every hour on the hour,
loud reminder of time passing
yet so rhythmic
to be heard, unacknowledged.
Discreet reminder on the half hour,
soft nudges when the big hand reaches 3, 6, 9.
The numbers,
—whether curvaceous or rectilinear—
in sets of 60—or 12
cookie-cutter shapes,
dutifully in their place,
predictable,
dependable,
in circle,
collectively hit,
60 times an hour
by the passing of time,
witness to public joys
and private pains.

Tick.Tock.Tick.Tock.
Have we come a long way
—or what?

Tick. Tock. Tick. Tock.

Wristwatch for everyone,
on every one.
Men, women.
Indispensable appendage.
Time.
All the time.
Whether status symbol
or lifeline,
space invasion,
through the wrist,
to the inner echo of Tick, Tock, Tick, Tock
—without chimes.
60 minutes reduced to 12 numbers—or 4
bars in between,
concentric bars,
anonymous representations
of the familiar curvaceous or rectilinear shapes
condensing time awareness from 60
to 12 cookie-cutter increments
dutifully in their place,
predictable,
inexorable,
in circle,
tracking the passing of time,
witness to public joys
and private pains.

Tick. Tock. Tick. Tock.
Have we come a long way
—or what?

3

Tock.Tick.Tock.Tick.

Digital tick
Digital tock.
Digital clock.
Standard time.
No more time
for personal time.
Anonymity of symbols.
Bars,
parallel bars,
perpendicular bars,
moving,
constantly,
in various trapping configurations,
dynamic mazes
moving, every minute,
every second,
allowing only the swift to find the exit
in time
for time.
Lying in wait,
we wait for the bars to line up
the next time around
hoping to find the exit,
in time,
for time.
But there is no time.
Time is now, with every Tick
and every Tock
of the clock,
witness to public joys
and private pains.

Tock.Tick.Tock.Tick.
Have we come a long way
—or what?

4

Tick. Tock. Tick. Tock.

Alarm clock.
Red alarm clock.
Alarming alarm clock.
Wake up call.
Wake-up!

It's time.
It's high time.
In the trapping of time
Let's find time
to find our self
and each other,
in a circle,
concentric,
accepting,
enjoying
the passing time
—curvaceous, rectilinear or digital—
celebrating
the individuality
and the integrity
of shapes,
—curvaceous, rectilinear or digital.
Let us regain control
of the invasion
of time
of space
of inner space.
It's about time.
It's all about time.

Tick. Tock. Tick. Tock.
Boom!

Will we come a long way
—or what?

• *Christine, 56* •

One night during a recent lecture by Gloria Steinem at Syracuse University, a female student in her twenties stood up at the podium during the question and answer period. She said that she had been raised in a family with four brothers and a father who was abusive to their mother as well as the children. She was concerned because she was noticing that her brothers were becoming abusive to their girlfriends and that all she knew to do was to talk to them about their behavior and to encourage the girlfriends to demand more respect. "I want to be a feminist," she said, "but I missed out on the women's movement and I don't know where to go to find out what to do."

Steinem smiled at her reassuringly, saying there was no mystique about feminism, that it was simply a way of looking at the world as if everyone mattered. She told the young woman that she was already acting as a feminist by doing what she could to address the issue, affirming her courage in confronting the brothers and speaking to their girlfriends about their right to respect.

In the course of the evening, several other young women stood up to say how isolated they felt, how it seemed that they had missed the boat to feminism, having been born as the Second Wave was crashing to shore. They longed for some sense of community, some structure of support they could lean into as they struggled to merge the personal and political in their own lives.

Each of them spoke of the women's movement in the past tense, like one might refer to the Suffragettes or the Abolitionists. Whatever they had heard and read about this movement appealed to them and they wanted to be part of it, but for them there was nothing to latch onto—just this hunger for something more, this craving for community.

Driving home that night, with their plaintive voices still in my mind, I remembered my early twenties, how hungry I was for the same thing, how lost I felt, and how everything changed when that wave of feminism washed over my life.

Before I found the women's movement, I never had a way of finding myself. At the age of twenty, when was dismissed from the convent, I was hurled into a world I had never prepared for. It was 1969 and in the two years I had been away, drugs, sex, and rock and roll had captured the attention of my generation. The times were a-changin and I had no idea how to fit into this culture that no longer felt like my own.

I moved to California, and with few marketable skills, it took a month to find a job. What little esteem I started with dwindled fast as the weeks went by. By the time the Bank of America hired me as a clerk typist for $80 a week, I was scraping the bottom for signs of self-worth.

I worked in an office with six other women, all of whom managed far better than I the demanding protocols of the working world. They were all comfortable in their mini-skirts, enlightened about hair and beauty products, and efficient at keeping their balance in those tall high heels we had to wear. I commuted by motorcycle thirty miles each way, arriving an hour before everyone else so I could curl my helmet-flattened hair, trade in sneakers for nylons and pumps, and change from my denims into prissy outfits I never felt right in.

Hungry for family and a sense of community, I tried desperately to squeeze my roundness into their perfect square. I never cared about the lunchroom chat, never could contribute to the boyfriend conversations, the diet talk, the beauty makeover discussions, but I sat there attentively while my heart ached for talk that mattered. None of us was content with who we were and we colluded in the myth that our worth was measured by the standards of others.

A few years went by before I heard of the women's movement and attended my first consciousness-raising group. The group had been meeting for a few weeks and I was surprised at their honesty, their careful listening and support of each other. I didn't speak much that first time, just introduced myself and said I had come looking for women with whom I had something in common. By the end of the evening, I felt at home with them.

I loved that they talked about their lives—not how to change them, but how to more fully express them—and that they were not concerned with weight or beauty or fashion, but with loving themselves exactly as they were.   We met week after week for two years, discussing whatever issues were surfacing in our lives. It always started with one woman sharing her experience and the rest of us adding our thoughts and feelings to the mix.

It was in this environment that I began to see the common patterns underlying our experience and learned the meaning of the term, "the personal is political." I had never understood politics as power before, never looked at my society from outside of it, scrutinizing it as one might scrutinize a foreign culture.

My training had always been that society was right and that if I didn't fit it, I was the one at fault. I had a civic duty to abide by the rules that everyone seemed to agree on. And beyond this, even more deeply embedded than society's law, was the law of the Church, the teaching that women were to serve, forego their own desires and needs, and defer to authority with humble docility.

Our group did not set out to challenge these teachings, but simply to share our experiences. The goal was to speak about our lives and to address the barriers that separated us from our dreams. As we spoke of the things we had been taught in our families, our churches, our schools, it became more and more apparent that it was these teachings that led to our lack of freedom, our lack of courage and confidence in our abilities.

As we explored our relationships with the church, with men, with other women, as we talked about sexuality, spirituality, money, jobs—in every area we had common experiences. In a room of eight women, each woman had a story to tell about being sexually harassed. Six women had been raped and blamed themselves on some level. Each lesbian had been disowned or discredited by her family when she came out. Each of us was making less money than our male co-workers. Each had felt some form of discrimination in our churches. And each of us tended to blame ourselves when we experienced rejection or loss.

None of us knew how to express anger, to assert ourselves confidently, to ask for what we wanted in our personal relationships without feeling selfish. We each had a desire to be creative, but none of us believed we had any skill in this area, though we wrote poetry, composed music and painted and drew and sang.

When I began to realize that it wasn't just me, that all the women in my group had grown up believing the same messages—that there were these prescribed roles we were supposed to perform and if we didn't do our part, there was something wrong with us—then it became possible to take a different look at those messages and see whether I wanted to accept or reject them.

Not only did that group offer a sense of community and support, it gave me a means to see my world from a new perspective, and to see myself as a person with new choices and new opportunities for self-expression. I no longer felt a victim or a casualty of my culture, but more a creator of my life, more willing to reach out and try new things.

As I look back on it now, I see that who I am as a woman, as an artist, was definitively shaped by that whole experience. The women's movement provided a place for my unfolding, a safe place where I could express myself and feel kindly received. In that context, I had the freedom to name myself, to say who I was under all the social trappings, and to emerge from those trappings like a butterfly from a chrysalis. The women I sat with in all those circles were midwives to my rebirth, as I was to theirs.

That night at the university, it broke my heart to hear those young women speak of their isolation, asking what happened to that wave and where should they go now to find community and sisterhood. And all I know to say to them is that sisterhood is not ready-made, not a treasure we go in search of, but something we create as we circle together and share our lives. It is an offshoot of intimacy, a state of being that does not precede but rises up from our listening and support of each other. As we share our stories, we are like the writers who write to learn what they think, the poets who write to learn what they feel. We cannot know what is in our depths until we have some way to unearth it, to express it in words or sounds or images. We cannot understand the mystery of our own lives until we have unconcealed them, like archeologists on a dig excavating our own histories.

As we say to each other who we are, what we have felt and feared, what we have dared, where we have been and where we are going, we learn to define ourselves from the inside out. In this process of revealing ourselves, we learn the art of creating ourselves. In listening to our own and each others' stories, we begin to see where we've been inhibited, how our choices have been compromised, our creativity stifled. We begin to see the ways we are bound by culture and tradition, nudged into our "appropriate roles" by church, state, and a marketing industry that provokes our insecurities in order to get us shopping for antidotes.

What has helped me stay true to my path is the stories of other women's journeys. I am encouraged over and over by their words which have managed to make their way through small presses, chapbooks, poetry readings and writers' conferences and spiritual gatherings and music fests and story-telling circles. Their words have blasted through thick walls of silence, years of yearning, and I draw my confidence from their truth and power.

In her introduction to *A Gift of Joy*, Helen Hayes writes, "We rely upon the poets, the philosophers, and the playwrights to articulate what most of us can only feel, in joy and sorrow. They illuminate the thoughts for which we only grope; they give us the strength and balm we cannot find in ourselves. Whenever I feel my courage waning, I rush to them. They give me the wisdom of acceptance; the will and resilience to push on."

And while this is true, it is also true that we do this for each other in the sharing of our stories, for our stories contain the answers to each other's questions. What I cannot find in searching through the riches and rubble of my own life may become apparent to me in the witnessing of yours.

In the passing on of our stories, we gift each other with the power of possibility. When I watch you claim your life and go after your dream, I begin to believe I can do it, too. When I see what you risk to achieve what you want, I think that I, too, could take that chance. When I hear what you have suffered while I see you trudging forward, I believe I can make it to the other side of my own darkness. What can save us if it is not our stories, not the careful sharing of who we are and what we dream for a world whose future rests in our hands?

• Jan, 51 •

Each of us contains a multitude of memories about growing up in a culture obsessed with a one-dimensional, skin deep kind of beauty. Though the facts of our stories are unique, the feelings and experiences are often universal.

As little girls we learn early on what is beautiful and what is not. We pick up messages from everywhere—from our mothers and fathers, our siblings, the movies and television shows we watched, the magazines and books we read, the advertisements that crept into our consciousness from everywhere, invited or not.

Our opinions about beauty have been shaped by the culture we live in, imprinted on our minds by many who are interested, not in the well-being of women, but in the profits to be garnered from our dissatisfaction with our bodies. And for the longest time, women have colluded in this. We have taken in the messages, judged ourselves against impossible standards, and paid dearly in money, time, and effort trying to "fit into" the *au courant* size of the day. And when we don't fit in, we feel dis-ease, discontent, disappointment with ourselves.

This dis-ease has escalated into actual disease for millions of women who are more obsessed with weight than health, who care less about fitness than what size they fit into, who see beauty in physical terms alone and with the narrowest of lenses. Untold numbers of women are dying to be thin, forfeiting their precious lives to a fantasy figure created by various individuals who rule the beauty and fashion industries and reap huge financial rewards from the self-hate of women.

In the history of our culture, women have achieved freedom from a variety of tyrannies. We have gathered together in circles during times of crisis and change, whispering our fears, sharing our feelings, finding ourselves in each other's stories until the commonness of our inner experience surfaced crystal clear against the outer chaos. And knowing we are not alone makes all things possible—including the recovery and reclamation of our own lives and passions.

It is in this spirit that we share these stories written by women of all shapes and colors and sizes and ages. They are a revelation of our culture, an unraveling of the strands of thought and images and words that have bound us over the years to a concept of beauty that has served us poorly.

Like shards of a broken mirror, these stories reflect a history that need not repeat itself. Assembled together, they illumine our strengths and our collective will to create a culture of acceptance for our children and grandchildren. These women have broken the silence; now let us circle together and break with the past. Let us take our courage from these voices, share our stories, and shape a new definition of beauty that includes us all.

10

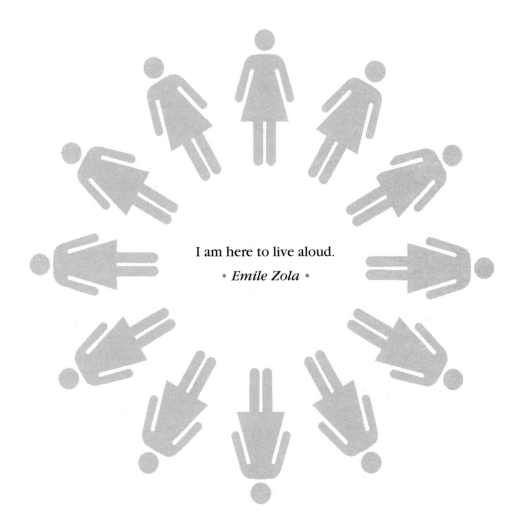

I am here to live aloud.

· *Emile Zola* ·

A CIRCLE OF WOMEN

The Ice Cream Cone

It was late afternoon, about 4 or 5 o'clock, and the sun fell slantingly across the girl's face as she ambled slowly home, kickball tucked under one arm, slowly licking a double vanilla ice cream cone from the store near the school. She liked to stay late and play kickball after school, and sometimes she would treat herself to an ice cream cone on the way home. Chocolate was certainly more interesting, deeper, more complex; but there was something about the cool whiteness of the vanilla against her tongue that she had always favored.

This year she had been chosen captain of the sixth grade kickball team—the first girl ever to have been chosen. Even though a few of the boys in class were as tall as she was, she could still run faster than any of them. When she ran, she just ran, she didn't think about her breasts bouncing, or whether sweat was running down her back; she just ran to beat the footsteps that had never managed to catch her.

She was the only one in her class to have breasts and hips and to have started her period. Most of the time she didn't think about those things, except sometimes boys would look at her in a certain way that was exciting, that made her run more slowly. At home, her parents said she needed to lose weight, and had taken her to the doctor to get a diet. That was last year, when she was 10. Every Sunday after breakfast, Dad would weigh her. She dreaded Sunday mornings, because she never seemed to lose weight, and the look of disappointment on her parents' faces was difficult to bear. Sometimes on Saturday night, she would sneak into the bathroom and play around with the scales until they would weigh a pound or two lighter. Then her parents were pleased and she was free for another week.

A few blocks from home, the girl slowed her steps slightly, the ice cream cone half gone. Her thoughts were on dinner and reading in her room later. The sound of a car slowing down made her turn around, and she saw her mother in the family car, slowing down to offer her a ride. The girl saw her mother's expression change when she saw the ice cream cone, and the car sped up and drove off, leaving the girl standing on the sidewalk. All thoughts of cool vanilla vanished. All thoughts of running like the wind disappeared as the girl threw the rest of the ice cream cone into the bushes and trudged the rest of the way home.

• *Laurie, 50* •

I Am Learning

I am 5 or 6 at the dinner table in the kitchen of our duplex in Newport, Kentucky. Out the window, beyond the railroad tracks, the sun, setting behind York Street School where my father attended before me, makes the building look aflame. My mother has served peas, a vegetable I do not like, so I refuse to eat them. My father and my older sister have finished and left the table. My mother admonishes before she retreats to the living room, "Stay there until you eat those peas." When she climbs the stairs, I stick my tongue out as far as I can and cross my eyes, then slump back in my chair with my arms folded across my chest.

Though I am fearful of my mother's anger, I am also a strong willed child. I do not like peas, especially not these stone-cold, gray-green paste wads that I push around my plate for more than an hour until I fall asleep on my folded arms at the table. "Judi!" my mother screams as she descends the stairs, "Eat those peas or get a spanking! It's nearly bedtime." The sky is dark with scattered stars that resemble spilled glitter. I have been there almost three hours.

"I'll take the spanking," I say. In a fury my mother tromps back up the stairs, and soon my father comes down with a Hi-Lo paddle, the kind that comes with a rubber ball attached to a string in its middle, a child's toy that in our house was a tool of punishment. My father doesn't want to spank me, he says, but I think he is afraid of my mother. He tries to talk me into eating the peas, tries cajoling, tries reasoning, but I refuse. Finally he does my mother's bidding and lays me over his knees and spanks me. I don't cry. I am learning to do battle over food.

* * * * * * *

Late summer smells—of roses too-heavy on their stems, and watermelon and thunderstorms and earth plowed under and mothballs. My sister, my mother, and I spend a morning in the attic going through boxes of winter clothes which had been packed the previous spring. It's a little like a treasure hunt, pulling out a favorite skirt and finding it can be lengthened to fit. And disappointing too when that dress I never liked of my sister's now fits me. It is the prelude to a shopping excursion where the vacancies in our closets will be filled with new colors and fabrics.

We are off to Swifton Shopping Center after sorting through the box of last year's school clothes. My sister is in the front seat. The favored position in that old '51 Plymouth is given to her for this trip in spite of the fact that I "finny-ed" it first. My mother is mad. At me. Again. She is mad at me so often that trying to separate one reason from another is like trying to unknot the silver chain that has lain too long in my jewelry box.

The parking lot is crowded, and we circle a few rows, my mother's anger circling too, a buzzard looking for a meal. I sit in the corner of the back seat trying to be invisible in the hope she'll lose her mad. Finally she gives up on finding a close spot and parks three quarters of the way down a row.

"Come on," she matter-of-facts to Barbara as I wait for my sister to get out so I can plop the seat forward and work my own way out to follow them. "Not you," my mother says, not looking at me. "I don't want to be seen with a fat girl. Stay here until we get back." And my mother slams her door and locks it, and the two of them leave.

In the melee of anger, forsakenness, insecurity, and disappointment, I tell myself over and over, It's not you. It's her. She's just mad again. It's not you. You didn't do anything. It's not you. It's her. It becomes a chant until they return. My sister's laughter stops as she approaches the car and waits for the door to be unlocked.

All the way home, my mother feigns conversation in Everything's-all-right tones, in Didn't-we-have-fun tones, in Isn't-she-sorry-she-couldn't-go-with us tones. Barbara answers when spoken to directly but is self-conscious with my mother's singular attention now that she is in the close quarters of the car with me. I refuse to let either of them see me hurt, so I adopt indifference, scrutinizing everything out the window for the ride home which seems three times as long as the ride to the shopping center. I slide into the crevice between the seat and its back like a lost coin, a scrap of paper, a bit of lint, hoping they would sense a Judi-shaped hole in their happy world.

At home, as they open bags and flounce new skirts and blouses and ooh and aah, I go to the bedroom I share with my sister, where I pretend their chatter comes from the neighbor's apartment. I don't cry, though my mother's disapproval is a bitter soup I try to stay afloat in. I am learning that others can be embarrassed by my body.

* * * * * * *

By eighth grade, I have outgrown my mother, who is 4 feet 11 inches tall and wears a size 7 dress. My sister, always the scrawny one, still wears my mother's hand-me-downs, but I have grown taller and more bosomy though my first bra, a 34 B, is still a year coming. "You look pregnant," my mother says when she hands me my first rubber girdle. "Aren't you ashamed to look like that? Wear this!" And so I do, despite the embarrassing popping and snapping as I peel down the girdle at school in the girls' restroom or in the gym locker room. I cough and sniff and clear my throat, flush the toilet repeatedly in the hope of

14

concealing the sound. I am learning to be embarrassed of my body.

*　*　*　*　*　*　*

One year ago, at the age of 51, I entered therapy with a woman who specializes in eating disorders because I am grossly obese and in danger of being at least crippled by the weight I carry. I am learning how deep the root system of my disorder is, and I am tracing its growth over the years. In so doing, I am also learning to take charge of—and most importantly, to accept—myself.

Most of my therapist's clients suffer from anorexia or bulimia, those devastating illnesses that are murdering our young women. Once as I was leaving the office, one of these young women, about 15, wearing black jeans and a black long-sleeved shirt, was sitting on the floor of the waiting room, leaning against the wall with her knees drawn up near her chest. She was so thin she looked like the capital letter N. As the therapist and I walked through the doorway, she glanced toward us, saw me, and lowered her head. She and I are like two penitents, the one entering the confessional who will not look directly at other and the one leaving who sees everyone with a clearer heart. I said hello to her, but she merely mumbled as she slid up the wail, passed by me and greeted the therapist directly.

I know I represent what she most fears about herself. I understand this, though it's a role I'm not happy to play. There was a profound sadness about our non-meeting, the two of us at opposite ends of the long knotted rope of eating disorders and having more in common, probably, than either of us might expect.

What I hope is that I live long enough for her to be able to look me in the eyes.

I hope she does.

• *Judi, 52* •

The Sabbath Meal

I was raised in an Orthodox Jewish household. During the week my brother and sister and I ate dinner at 5 o'clock. My mother sipped on a martini during our dinner. She and my father ate dinner alone later, with the kids banned from the dining room.

The two main Sabbath meals were dinner on Friday evening and lunch on Saturday after synagogue. We ate together as a family. We were all dressed up in our Sabbath clothes, clean and pressed. The table was always covered with a heavily starched white tablecloth. We were a "perfect" family sitting around a beautiful table. My mother always prided herself on our beauty and cleanliness. Shoes were polished. Hair was combed to perfection.

Prayers and blessings always accompanied these meals. The meals were filled with religious rituals. We had permanent seats at the table. We were never to sit in my father's seat at the head of the table. His seat was holy and was never even to be touched. My mother sat at the other side of the rectangular glass table designed to seat six. I sat next to my father on one side of him. My older brother sat on the other side.

The younger twins, a boy and a girl, sat on either side of my mother. The Sabbath meals usually lasted about two hours. It began with Kiddush, the blessing over the sacred wine, followed by the ritual of hand washing, and followed by more prayers and blessings. The meal started out with challah, the traditional braided Sabbath bread. At the center of the table were the sacred candlesticks. They were handed down from my grandmother to my mother. They would be handed down to me in the future, as the oldest daughter.

Between each of the courses, we sang traditional hymns praising G-d and the sanctity of the Sabbath. No one was ever allowed to leave the table until the meals were over and the final blessings chanted. And none of us children ever dared to leave the table. The only one who left was my mother. After the main course, my mother always left the table. The meal was incomplete. Dessert had not been served yet, and we were required to sit silently until my mother returned to the table to serve the final course.

Although my parents' bathroom was down the hall, the noises that came from there were so loud, that it was impossible not to hear my mother retching. We silently remained in our assigned seats gazing at my mother's empty chair. No one ever spoke. We sat listening to the sounds of my mother throwing up her food. We were told that she had a very sensitive stomach and that "aggravation" precipitated these bouts of vomiting. I remember feeling very guilty.

I was not very well behaved. I had what was called a "big mouth" and was always being fresh and talking back to my mother. I felt sure that I was the main cause of my mother's "sensitive stomach." A few minutes after the excruciating retching noises died down, my mother would return to her seat. She then gave out dessert, which was usually a small portion of red Jello (Kojel— kosher gelatin), with a piece of a canned peach artfully placed inside the Jello. We would silently eat this final course. My mother just sat in her chair gazing at us. She didn't complete the meal with us. My father would say to her, "Aren't you having any?" And she'd say, "No. I've already had my dessert."

I never knew that my mother was bulimic until two weeks before her death from cancer at age 69. I walked into her sickroom to find her making herself vomit. "What are you doing, Mom??? What the hell are you doing?" I cried in horror. She said, "It doesn't matter anymore. It just doesn't matter anymore."

My mother died two weeks after she told me about her lifelong eating disorder and struggles with her weight and her body and her incessant desire to be "thin and beautiful." I wasn't present at the moment of her death, but I was told that at the end she vomited profusely and then died.

All four of us children got something that was hers after her death. I got the candlesticks and the bulimia.

• *Malkah Leah, 50* •

I smile. Lips pulled back, eyes shining out of the crinkled little slits that my pushed-up smiling cheeks have made. Teeth flashing—all of them—because that's how big my smile is most times. And the world smiles back an affirmation of what my mirror sees. "Yeah, Rainelle," it says, "You're okay." Okay. Finally. That's something, I think as I reflect on the metamorphosis I had undertaken to achieve this appearance that so many find pleasing.

Like most people, I was born with aesthetic imperfections. As I grew and developed, they not only became more apparent, but were also magnified by comparison to my siblings and cousins—big feet, wide nose, short neck, a certain amount of "heaviness," and worse still, big gapped teeth. This "ugliness" read as a testimony to my mother's imperfection, and an indictment of my own character.

"How did that one turn out so ugly?" a neighbor asked when sizing up me and my twin brother. "Looks like she must be the bad one," strangers assessed. My mother's reaction was a litany of frustrating attempts to correct what she had made wrong. "Hold your head up off your shoulders. Keep pinching your nose, maybe it'll get narrower. Don't laugh, don't smile, makes you even uglier...."

I went to school pinching my nose, craning my neck and pursing my lips against the event of a laugh or smile, but the list only grew: "Oh, dear, what's wrong with your hair?" my second grade teacher asked in horror when an unexpected rainfall revealed its true nappy texture that my mother had always so painstakingly masked with hot pressing combs and hair straighteners.

I carried what I had learned about acceptance into adulthood: acceptance equals not looking like me. And I spent a good part of adulthood trying to create an acceptable appearance: makeup, dieting, bulimia, corsets, straightening combs, hair relaxers, never smiling and vowing to save enough money to buy perfect teeth. Some of it worked. Men told me I looked good, and I dated them. Always because they chose me, not because there was anything particular about them that I liked. Got married even. For the same reason.

Had kids, divorced, and the cycle continued. It translated into the rest of my life, too: a career that I had not particularly chosen, but was grateful to have been accepted for, bosses I didn't particularly like—disliked sometimes—but gratitude when they showed some acceptance, the same with friends. I settled into a neighborhood that was all wrong, but it accepted me and my children. And into a life of acceptance that I didn't like, learned to accept, and struggled to maintain. Until my child grew old enough to face that same world.

It's funny how kids can open your eyes when you think they're already open.

The same culture that had pressed upon me the urgency to look good enough, be pleasing enough, was now teaching my teenage son to do the same—and it could cost him his life. It all boiled down to acceptance or my child. I chose my child.

That was ten years ago. Never did get those perfect teeth. Today, ten years wiser, ten years content, I look down at my feet, and am thankful that they're big enough to hold this big strong body and take it where it needs to go. My neck is still short, and I'm glad that it keeps my head close to my heart, where it should be. And my hair, a thick healthy mass of nappy dreadlocks growing unsculpted, uninterrupted in their own direction, like me—into whatever they're supposed to become.

I no longer seek acceptance, but to be myself, and I know that it is the reason why so many people feel that they must have met me before somewhere; who find my look comfortable, easy to be with. Familiarity is a natural attraction.

"You have such a beautiful smile," I am often told. And I laugh at the irony of having spent half a lifetime hiding the part of me that is most attractive.

• *Rainelle, 50* •

When I Was Young

When I Was Young
I
used to cover my face
except for my eyes
I could imagine myself
beautiful
I
became
many things
just looking
into my own eyes
they were windows to the underworld
to regions
galaxies
lands far, far away
distant places
altered realities
gardens
fairies
dragons
they were my time travel machine
my escape
from the harsh reality
of my present existence
I
could be anything
I
wanted to be
my heart's desire
uncover my face though
and the dreariness
the heaviness returned
the fears
self-loathing ever present
the self I saw
deep in those ice blue eyes
trapped
forgotten
unwanted

• *Lynn, 36* •

Food

Food is my drug of choice. It is my friend, my enemy, my reward, as well as the club with which I beat my body for betraying me so deeply.

Food is the final frontier—it is in my relationship with food that I will finally begin to reconnect with the body I've refused to inhabit for so long. Food is the route in. Coming to some accommodation with it is the way out.

Food has been my shield—sugar and carbos—softening the edges, still there for me when I was finally able to leave the alcohol behind. Food provides the insulation for my raw nerve endings—it prevents mind and body from flying apart under the pressure as the tectonic plates of my being and destiny grind against each other.

Food has been a cheap fix, but I fear it is becoming a costly comfort. I don't know how much longer my body will be able to carry around the extra weight without a serious malfunction.

I remember when I dieted in my twenties—renouncing the pleasure of eating what I wanted for the false sense of control afforded by "exchange units," every bite planned for, weighed, and measured. I remember how light and free I felt without the layers of fat weighing me down. I also remember how exposed and vulnerable thin felt to me, how scared I was. A dizzy combination of fragility and freedom—the sense of knowing boundaries and edges in the physical plane—a knowing that would take me decades to reach in emotional and spiritual dimensions. Being thin was a mix of exhilaration and terror.

That first "thin" experience was one of my first steps away from victimhood. In the intervening years, I've been learning how to be in charge of other parts of my life, and as I've been working hard on the intangibles, the visible has slipped away, so far away that I wonder if I will ever get it back. It is not about appearance. It is about choices. It is about "relinquishing attachment." If I want to feed my spirit I will have to alter the way I feed my body. I will have to shift my attitudes and find other ways to feed myself.

I have been learning how to take care of myself spiritually and emotionally. I have more tools at my disposal now than I did 25 years ago. Now I need to focus my awareness on what feeds my spirit. Then maybe, just maybe, I can find the courage to cross this "final frontier" in my relationship with food, another step on the journey back into my body.

• Judith, 48 •

My Mom was on a diet my whole life! In the last 20 years I have lost 4,000 pounds, yet I still weigh 200 pounds. I have tried every diet, program, supplement, and gimmick with great success, and I have such a pretty face. Mom always wanted me to lose weight, and so I did—only to gain it back again. I really don't feel fat until I go to my closet or look in the mirror.

Last week I started a "new" exercise class; the instructor seemed surprised that I am so athletic and flexible, my blood pressure is normal, my energy is off the charts, and yet...Oh please bring back the renaissance women!! Why do I continue to worry and fret about my weight? Because my mom said I would be happier. How much happier can I be? I have two wonderful daughters, the love of my life, an exciting career, and the home of my dreams.

My mom lost her memory and forgot me and that I am fat and to her dying day she wondered whether or not she was allowed to eat certain things. I am afraid I have done the same to my daughters! Please forgive me and my Mom!

• Penny, 55 •

I'm 5 feet 2 inches tall and have shoulders as wide as a Green Bay Packer football player. At least, that's what my brother told me year after year as I was growing up. If we were in the kitchen together, he often curled his arms out to his sides and stomped on the hardwood floor like a gorilla, ostensibly imitating how I looked and walked. I believed him.

As a result of his teasing comments and pantomimes, as well as my mother's calling me her "dear fat daughter" whenever I reached for a cookie or potato chip, I saw myself as a BIG girl. Wide and heavy. Fat.

Did I really look like that? No. Sure, I was a little overweight, about ten pounds worth, and my hips and thighs were bigger than any young girl would want them to be, but I was not the size of a football player. I just didn't know that. For years, I removed the shoulder pads from every blouse, sweater, and jacket I bought. It didn't matter that most of those items were a size small; I still viewed myself as big. As I grew older, I started to see the truth, but it was a slow process. Since my negative self-image had been developed over many years, changing it would not happen over night.

Eventually, I stopped listening to my brother and mother, and I started hearing what other people had to say.

"You're small."

"I wish I could fit into your clothes."

"You have beautiful eyes."

"You have a great smile."

The list goes on, but it took me a long time to hear those positive comments. Even longer to believe them. I stopped judging myself so harshly and started paying attention to how shoulder pads helped me stand taller, squared off some-what rounded shoulders, and made my waist look smaller. I stopped looking in the mirror with such a critical eye. Instead of focusing on the individual nega-tive aspects of myself—from my hips to the little mole on my face—I began seeing the overall person.

I stopped comparing myself to other people. I may have wanted a long, lithe, ballet dancer's body, but I finally realized it would be a physical impossibility. I couldn't change the body-type I'd been born with; I could, however, learn which clothing styles would flatter my assets and conceal my hips.

Most of all, I stopped disliking myself, stopped making myself miserable because of unrealistic self-views and other people's negative comments. I concentrated on the good things I discovered about myself—my intelligence, my sense of humor, the muscular, athletic power in my thighs, and many more things. With each discovery, my self-esteem rose. I felt good about myself. I still do.

• Ann, 41 •

Blue

The mountain is blue tonight,
This means rain tomorrow.
Rain tomorrow means,
I can't wear my dress.
Can't wear my dress means,
I won't look the way I want to.
Won't look the way I want to means,
I won't feel right about myself.
Won't feel right about myself means,
I won't have confidence.
Won't have confidence means,
I'll avoid going where you might see me.
Avoid going where you might see me means,
I'll stay home.
Stay home means,
I'll eat.
Eat means,
I'll get fat.
Get fat means,
I won't have confidence.
Won't have confidence means,
I won't feel right about myself.
Won't feel right about myself means,
I'll avoid seeing you.
Avoid seeing you means,
I'll have nothing to look forward to.
Have nothing to look forward to means,
I'll eat.
Eat means,
I'll get fat.
Get fat means,
I'll never see you.
Never see you means,
You'll be with someone else.
Be with someone else means,
I'll be alone.
Be alone means,
I'll have nothing to live for.
Nothing to live for means,
I'll eat.
Eat means,

I'll get fat.
Get fat means,
I won't have confidence.
Won't have confidence means,
I won't feel right about myself.
Won't feel right about myself means,
I can't wear my dress.
Can't wear my dress means,
Rain tomorrow.
Rain tomorrow means,
The mountain is blue tonight.

• *Hannelore, 55* •

We moved to St. Louis, Missouri the summer before my seventh grade year began, and I was miserable. My family had moved to St. Louis from a small, friendly little town just southeast of St. Louis, about 60 miles from the city. I had been so happy there with good friends and great fun in school and at the city pool in the summer. I was so sad to leave everyone behind.

When the first day of school arrived, the hugeness of the junior high school overwhelmed me. I was ignored and shoved from one class to another in the herd of students changing classes. The days that followed were lonely, and my unhappiness grew. Each day at lunch, I sat alone and ate corn chips, a Hostess cupcake, and chocolate milk. Each day my lunch was the same. I'd come home after school and eat the same thing before dinner. I'd snack after dinner. My waistline grew.

Mom and I were sitting at the kitchen table one Saturday. I was feeling rejected and confused because I had such good memories of the friends and life I had to move away from only months ago. I said, "Nobody likes me. No one talks to me at school. I hate it here, Mom."

Mom was busy fixing lunch. I went on, "The boys don't even know I exist and there's a dance coming up. I won't go. No one will ask me." Mom was listening to me with a half ear, but she heard the part about boys. Mom said, "Well, boys don't like fat girls."

I was devastated. I cried out, "Mom!"

"Well, its true," my mother said as she left the kitchen to do something in another part of the house. I sat at the kitchen table, stunned and hurt. Tears welled up in my eyes and trickled down my checks. Finally, I was reduced to sobbing quietly so Mom wouldn't hear. I went to my bedroom and looked in the mirror. I felt huge, and the reflection in the mirror loomed in my mind. Looking back, I was perhaps 10 pounds overweight, but it might as well have been 50 or 60 pounds the way I perceived myself after Mom's words.

To this day, I'll never know what possessed Mom to say such a thing to me. I've long since forgiven her, but I remember how much it stung.

Later in school, boys did notice me, I dated often and went to many dances. I had slimmed down to the point of being underweight. Was it Mom's statement that led to the weight loss? I don't know, looking back. I just know how very hurt I was.

Now I am a mature woman and have two grown daughters that are 17 and 21 years old. I would never, ever say such a statement to them. Because after all these years, the words still make me tear up at the very thought of the humiliation I felt. I'm more concerned that my daughters feel okay about themselves and their appearance than what boys don't like.

• Judith, 43 •

Living at home was hard enough, but living close to my parents in later years meant surrendering to the barrage of criticism aimed at me. My parents were first-generation Americans. Their childhood of poverty, illness, and responsibility brought them to adulthood during the depression years. They were no-nonsense kind of people, not big on feelings. Not exactly sensitive to the "overly sensitive," as they called me…among other things. Those other things pertained to my looks and intelligence. I was to be measured by my prospects for marriage. In short, what attributes did I possess that would make me a valuable wife?

As a child, helping my grandmother prepare Sunday dinner won me parental approval. What a good wife I would be someday, even though I was not pretty! I was a good cook and I had a nice disposition. Was this not a compliment? My siblings had named me "Horse." They said it with such disdain. This too was confusing. I did not see an ugly girl when I looked in the mirror. While they thought I was fat and I believed them, I did not see a fat girl in the mirror.

Looking at old photographs, I am always surprised to see the thin child I was, except for a year or two just before puberty. I did not resemble a horse. But I was big-boned, and by the time I was 12, I was taller than the four other females in my family. That was no great feat however, as my mother was 4 feet 9 inches, and my oldest sister exactly 5 feet on her eighteenth birthday. Nevertheless, I was always conscious of certain things. People saw me as big and ugly, my mother ate Hershey bars at night after everyone had gone to bed, no one cared that my grandmother had big breasts and flabby arms, and I was not going to get a husband being a big fat horse.

At 16, I was slender and attractive. My grandmother's Mongolian bloodline was at the roots of my long dark hair. My boyfriend thought me beautiful. That is what mattered most to me, even if my folks didn't like him. The talk of physical looks ceased for a while, although the attack on my intelligence remained. So I stopped listening to my family.

Body criticism lay dormant, raising its ugly head in later years when I lived far from home and would only visit once in a while. It came full force on the advent of my pregnancy. I was diagnosed with a thyroid condition and severe water retention. Medication was prescribed by my doctor, and I gained 28 pounds. This was not considered far from the norm in the late 1970s. In my mother's day, pregnant women (at least those who went to doctors and hospitals) were not supposed to gain more than 5 to 10 pounds. I would have been considered a low birth-weight baby by today's standards. My baby weighed 8 pounds at birth. My pregnancy and weight gain disturbed my family. Weird how people confuse pregnancy with obesity.

After my child was born I returned to my normal weight, but over the 21 years since, my weight has increased. Now in menopause, still taking thyroid medication, I am struggling with weight fluctuation. I do not like the bloating or my clothes being tight, but I do not mind actually being heavier now. I feel more grounded with the extra padding. So I get the next size. I'm comfortable, and still look good when I look in the mirror. A long time ago I stopped caring about what appealed to people I didn't know. I cared about what appealed to me and to the people in my life. Some people, men or women, are offended by bigger, fatter women, or intimidated by extra pounds. Sometimes other people's reactions make me feel self-conscious, but most of the time I don't even think about it.

• Anin, 51 •

Body Story

In her family its history was silenced
though body became,
even in absence, something
of shame.

Nice people
didn't have one, not her father
surely, and her mother
only fleetingly,
once a month behind closed doors.

But she grew one right enough,
a mountainous body magnificent
in its longings,
insistent as a fishwife who lolls about the house
like a large, unfettered scrawl.

She was a letter they had written to themselves
then put aside,
delivered now years later by the round hand
of their desire:

Dear Ones.

I am the memory of an August afternoon
your bodies, like the late summer
lush in the ripe heat. Remember,
re-member me, waiting in the rush and ache of August
deep in the heavy fruit
like an incomprehensible seed.

• *Karen, 59* •

The Girdle, a Woman's Best Friend

My mother always wanted me to be thin and beautiful. She taught me a great deal about how to accomplish this. There were many rules and regulations to be followed to achieve this goal. I was taught at a very young age that managing money correctly was also essential. I was trained to be thrifty, to save money, and to buy only things that were on sale. But there was one area of our lives as women where money was no object.

"You never try to save money on a girdle," my mother taught me. "Your girdle is your best friend. Always buy the best." I will always remember our shopping trips to Sears. We went to that particular department store because they not only sold the best Playtex rubber girdle in town, but they had a professional woman to fit you and make sure that you bought the correct size. It was of little value to have an excellent girdle if the fit was not right. My mother and I would usually hold hands as we walked into that special women's department in the back of the store. She would rush in to find the saleswoman who really knew all about the fitting of girdles and say, a little too loudly for my adolescent ears, "I want my daughter to have the best Playtex rubber girdle. I don't care how much it costs. And I want you to find a really firm longline bra for her to wear with it."

My mom and I waited in the dressing room for the saleslady to come in. I felt really embarrassed about taking off my clothes in front of this strange woman. But she was a professional, like a doctor. There were a lot of years that I mildly protested, but always gave in at the end, because my mother had my own good in mind. It was always a struggle to pull the girdles up. Apparently the correct fit meant a moderate amount of difficulty pulling the girdle up over my hips, but when it was in place, I could look in the mirror and see a significant difference in my form.

The correct fit seemed to be as tight as I could tolerate it, and still be able to breathe. There was always fat that got pushed up and hung over the girdle, but there was a ready solution to that as well. The longline bra with the stiff bones compressed the fat hanging over the stomach. Of course, there was a limit to this miracle makeover, and there always appeared to be some excess fat hanging over the top of the longline bra in the back, but that part had limited visibility to others, so it didn't matter.

Pulling off the rubber girdle was always difficult. I would sweat profusely in the hot little dressing room, and the girdle would stick to me. My mom carried a little bottle of Johnson's baby powder in her purse at all times. She taught me that if I powdered myself first, the girdle would go up easier. She was right. The powder was also good to cover up the red marks that the bones of the corset left on my young, sensitive skin.

My mother and I always left Sears with a few bags filled with perfectly fitting bras and girdles. I wore them all the time, except when sleeping at night. My mother taught me that a lady never leaves the house without a good fitting girdle. She trained me to put the girdle on as soon as I got up in the morning. One never knew if a friend or traveling salesman might knock on the door and come into the house. "No one should see a woman without her girdle on," my mother told me countless times. If we were out somewhere and my mother saw the behind of a woman looking girdle-less, she would never hesitate to point out to me the "looseness" of that woman. She would call her names and make deprecating remarks about the way this woman cared for her body. A woman without a girdle was like a woman walking around naked in public.

I didn't have many dates as a teenager, but occasionally a boy would ask me out to the movies. I always took advantage of every opportunity I had to go on a date, although there was a special problem that I had when I did so. Luckily, my mother had a solution to this all figured out and taught me how to deal with this problem. When I sat for an extended period of time in a movie theater, the tightness of the girdle, in conjunction with the tightness of the longline bra, seemed to compress my abdomen to such an extent that I would get excruciating stomach pains. There would be a huge build-up of gas that could not escape. The optimal solution to this problem was a cup of hot tea followed by lying down on my stomach, which allowed the gas to escape, due to the straightening out of my body. The length of time in the seated position necessary to watch a whole movie was far too long for normal expulsion of the gas pockets. Of course, there was no hot tea to drink in the movie theater, but I was able to go to the bathroom and lie down on the floor three or four times during the movie.

My mother told me that wherever I went, there would always be a women's bathroom to go to where I could lie down on the floor face down. This has always proven to be true. My mother taught me many lessons on how to be thin and beautiful. I have much to thank her for today.

• *Maxine, 50* •

When I was younger, I was a cheerleader…a princess on the prom court…a princess at a beauty pageant…a dancer…

And later on, after bringing a beautiful girl into the world, my body no longer looks like it once did…it made me cry.

Then I remembered when I was younger still…I thought that my grandmother was the most beautiful woman in the whole wide world with her ample breasts and soft, round stomach…

And my own mother is still so beautiful, even though she doesn't think so… And now, when I take baths with my little girl, she tells me how beautiful she thinks I am…

• *Naomi, 37* •

Brown

Brown socks. Brown shoes. Brown anklets and brown oxfords. My pre-adolescent feet embodied my self-image. They stood for the girl I believed I was, the person I was told I would be. In my formative years, I walked through the world as an ugly duckling. Pudgy, awkward, tummy protruding, hair parted efficiently in the middle and held aside with barrettes, I longed for a transformation I couldn't believe would come.

Pink tights. Pink toe shoes. Tutus and tiaras. Decorations decidedly not mine. My younger sister—slight, svelte, acrobatic and lithe—was the ballerina. She floated across wooden floors with only a barre to catch her; she drifted in front of mirrored walls. They validated the vision in pink she was.

And at the upright piano, angled toward an instructor who counted loudly, demonstrated steps, barked out orders for different moves, was my mother, the accompanist, offsetting the cost of lessons for my sister. While all the eyes were on my sister, I sat on a folding chair, watching, trying not to see in the mirror this pudgy, awkward, ugly duckling wearing brown socks, brown shoes.

Once, I asked my mother for dancing lessons too. I dreamt of being a swan, longed to shed those brown socks and shoes. "You?" she replied, her eyebrows lifting with a mix of disbelief and surprise. "You?" echoed in my soul, emphasizing the absurdity of my dream. I never asked again.

I struggle still with those proverbial 10 pounds. I always will, though perhaps not for the same reasons. I've befriended that pudgy, awkward little girl and love her dearly for all that she was and never could be.

Now, I indulge her fondness for fun socks and I buy her shoes, all kinds of shoes, any kind her heart desires—but brown. None are, will ever be, brown.

• *Noel, 50* •

35

I grew up in a family obsessed with the "correct" body image and physical appearance. I was the only child out of six who was overweight, and because of this was constantly taunted by my older brothers and their friends about my size. I grew up believing something was horribly wrong with me; I didn't fit in with the rest of my siblings, I was a bad person because I couldn't control myself and my eating habits. My mother would encourage me to lose weight in whatever way possible.

I was dieting from the age of 8. At age 12, I was anorexic and my parents were thrilled when I lost 40 pounds over a four-month period (they had no idea that anything was wrong—even when I did not menstruate for 9 months). At age 14, I had gained back those 40 pounds and more and was then prescribed amphetamines by a physician to assist me with my weight "struggles."

By age 16, I started bingeing and purging after reading about bulimia in a women's magazine popular at that time. No one ever asked me why I ate so much, no one wanted to listen to what I had to say or how I felt about things going on in my life that contributed to the bad feelings I had about myself. No, they just wanted to treat the symptom without understanding the underlying problem.

I know my parents only wanted me to be "happy" and they believed (and instilled in me the fact) that I could never be happy or satisfied if I was overweight. What I wish they would have instilled in me instead was the knowledge that people come in all shapes and sizes and that physical appearance is not the only attribute about a person that is important. I wish I had been taught about the satisfaction we can obtain from things like intellectual pursuits, having an open mind, understanding the uniqueness of each individual, and seeing the beauty of the world around us.

I feel that I wasted so much time focusing on what was wrong with my body and my looks (when in actuality nothing was really wrong). I regret spending all of that time that I could have instead spent developing my intellect, meeting new people, and exploring the exciting things in our world. I finally accepted my body and myself with the assistance of a kind, encouraging therapist and by reading and really taking to heart the works of author Geneen Roth. She helped me "break free" of all the false notions I had about weight loss. She helped me understand that we first have to accept ourselves as we are before we can move on to eventually lose weight.

No longer do I wake up on Mondays swearing to start a new diet, vowing to lose 10 pounds in 2 weeks. No longer do I feel guilty if I eat a piece of cake, a slice of lasagne, a roll with butter on it. Once I "broke free" of all the dieting nonsense, I had a lot more time to develop other aspects of myself that I had let go because of my preoccupation with my body image. I returned to college and obtained a second degree; I met people who were interesting and intelligent, people who were accepting of diversity and difference.

I have now learned to listen to my body and to fill it with nutritious foods that enable me to function at my best; I have learned that regular exercise also enhances my feeling of well-being. Would I change a part of my body if I had the resources to do so? Not now. I like the way I look and feel about myself. It took me a long time and a lot of work to be able to get to this place. I'm glad I made it. I'm glad I'm here.

• *Christy, 37* •

I entered the double bind of living in a woman's body when I was very young. I began menstruating when I was 9 and a half, which, in those days was almost unheard of. I looked different from my peers, I smelled different, I felt different. I had hips and breasts and thighs and body hair, and all the other girls my age were just that—girls. I tossed and turned in the moonlight, dreaming of kisses, of unknown yearnings. I certainly couldn't share these feelings within my family or with my friends—society viewed me as a child. Except I became aware of men's eyes on me, on my breasts and legs and thighs. I felt drawn to that attention and repelled by it at the same time.

My parents were determined that I stay a young girl, and so they focused on my curves as the root of the problem. I was 10 when I was first put on a diet. It has taken me 40 years to make an agreement with myself never to diet again, no matter what outer shape my body finds itself in. As a member of the dominant culture, I certainly have fitted into the blond/blue-eyed mold, but for many years I haven't weighed what that culture believes I should, and I have been all but invisible for all these years. I have been able to swim through crowds of people effortlessly, no eyes turning my way to examine my body, my face with interest. I realized that the double bind of age and weight have put me in the category of being considered someone most men would not consider dating.

This paradigm has allowed me to develop friendships with men, has allowed me to develop friendships with younger women as a mentor, but I sometimes see the disdain in the eyes of thinner women. For years I put off doing things like swimming "until I lost weight." Not any longer, and never again. Even if I am invisible in society, I will walk where I want to, eat what I want to, and take loving care of this body, not a someday body.

• *Laurie, 50* •

Beauty

"The quality or aggregate of qualities in a person or thing that gives pleasure to the senses or pleasurably exalts the mind or spirit..."

• *Merriam Webster Collegiate Dictionary* •

"Pretty is, as pretty does," my Mama would say to me as I misbehaved. Those words stopped me from my ugly endeavors because, as a little girl, if there was anything I wanted to be in my Mama's eyes, "pretty" was high on my list. Slowly I learned that Mama's idea of beauty meant that you behaved in a manner that was good from the inside out.

As time passed and I endeavored to fulfill my Mama's idea of beauty, I began to look at the women around me for ideas of the "beauty" I wanted to become. Pleasantly robust, with sparkling eyes, my Aunt Anita had a beauty that drew me in like a moth to the light. With a smile that could stop a man at 30 feet, milk chocolate skin and a charm that any person would want, I found in her my first role model for beauty at age 5.

I would watch this great aunt of mine, as she walked her beauty dance down the grocery store aisle. A confident woman, she smiled, and sometimes laughed at some story she shared with her only sister, Lu Emma, my other great aunt, as they shopped.

Just like me, other people were drawn to Aunt Anita because her confidence and warmth made them feel better by being in her presence. She had a way of not making other women jealous of her while men liked her subtle, friendly ways. And everyone appreciated her open heart that couldn't watch a person go without the necessities of living, like food, clothing, and shelter.

Maybe that's why she finally ended up a minister's wife, well taken care of by a doting husband who felt that he had found his special jewel in my Aunt Anita. Talking with her about men and life, following my divorce at 20 years of age, I discovered that the confidence and beauty that she had exuded all my life had come by way of some tough lessons. Her seasoning came via several marriages before she became the jewel in her last husband's life.

"You have to keep on trying until you get it right," she said to me. I knew she was talking about finding the right person to be in a relationship with, but I also took it to mean I had to keep on trying until I got being a woman right.

It was during Luisah Teish's portrayal of Sojourner Truth that I discovered my next beauty role model at age 26. Displaying Sojourner's strength, pride, and joy in being a woman, I felt that Teish possessed those qualities herself. Without these qualities how could she bring Sojourner so colorfully into being.

I ventured forward after her performance and introduced myself. This tall, brilliant, articulate, spirited woman greeted me like an old friend and made time to talk to me. I discovered the personality I had seen on the stage was only a small part of this amicable woman.

"When I find that I fear something, I crawl toward confronting it and test my courage bit by bit until I conquer the fear," Teish told me when I asked for her key to emulating that courage.

From Teish I learned that friendship could develop into kinship. I also learned that beauty demands a willingness to delve into the disordered depths of the self. Beauty includes finding the not-so-pretty parts of ourselves and bringing them to the light for healing.

A few months ago, a friend of mine, Hilda, was approached by a mutual friend to appear in a video she was making. Taken aback by the offer, Hilda could only think of reasons why she shouldn't be in the video. Luckily her age, gray hair, or size was not among her considerations as much as her long-time unexpressed feeling that she was not a beauty.

From her perceptive light brown eyes to laugh lines that are like the crevices of the earth, with an enduring smile and long gray locks flowing like waves reflecting the moon, Hilda is a spirited reflection of Obatala's humility, grace and wisdom. She cried when a few of us told her how beautiful she was. (Obatala is the Yoruba deity that holds the ethics and morality of the Ifa spiritual tradition. We learn to humble our egos and gain inner knowledge that leads to wisdom by following his precepts.)

Hers is not just the beauty of the ancient women of legend, whom men fought wars and lost kingdoms over. But more importantly, she is a woman whose beauty is an expression of a pure heart.

This kind of beauty is what I discovered through each phase of living, child and queen so far, as I look toward becoming crone. At each phase I gained insight into womanhood as beauty. What we all need to know at each phase is different because we are different at each new turn. Each of my beauty models have lived vastly different lives but share the common qualities of integrity, courage, wisdom, and they provide an illuminating foundation.

As black women, they give me examples to aspire to other than this society's popular images of ultra slim, noncolored, pubescent, un-feminine females. They are women who bring forth the images of the "queens of the earth" that black men were paying homage to in the 1960s; beautiful women who earned their beauty by learning life's lessons of courage and survival by accessing their natural spirit.

Mama was right…"Pretty is, as pretty does."

• *Uzuri, 46* •

Thinner

Thinner...

Isn't that what every woman wants?

I slim until I am sharp.
Sideways, I'm a double-edged razor,
all cutting surface.

Food has lost its savor for me.
My body craves
metal in the marrow,
steel in the gut.

I have become too hard to chew,
painful to swallow,
drawn out like attenuated strands
of angel hair pasta spooled on a fork
hiding constantine wire in their center.

This has made me thinner.
Less room to rattle around inside myself.
Less of me to be afraid.
Smaller target. Too late, already hit.

When I grow lightheaded,
I throw more fuel on the burner.
Just enough calories to keep going.

Always just enough.

Any more and I'll choke on it.
Any more and I'll raise my standards
of what is enough.

• Lea, 37 •

How I Grew to Be

One day I was practicing my golf swing at the driving range with my father, who knew I was 35 and obviously still single. He pointed out a cute guy, and said to me "Hey, maybe if you don't swing quite so hard, that guy will come over here and show you how to hit 'em."

I looked at him in blank astonishment. "You mean pretend I don't know what I'm doing so he'll feel like I need help and come over and talk to me? Dad, all my life you taught me to be strong and capable. Now you want me to fake incompetence so some stupid man will feel comfortable approaching me?"

Was he sorry now I learned so well? Had I learned the wrong lessons? My dad taught me karate alongside my year-older brother. "Hi-ya!" I shouted proudly, my red-bruised hand burning with pain. He took us both fishing, and bought us both our first rifles. He taught us the same—be strong, do not lie, cheat or steal. He loved us the same, and was scrupulous about treating us the same. He was a good man.

I was busy growing strong. Too proud to compromise my strength, I spurned heels, nylons, makeup and dresses. I despised the coquettish female games of man baiting. I was the bee, not the flower. Now, the beauty of women isn't in me but occasionally. On a good day.

When I see a beautiful woman, I am weak with admiration. But I am usually the admirer, not the admiree. I content myself with inner beauty, dreams of beauty and the beautiful woman who gives the love of her life to me.

• *Kathy, 40* •

I was raised in an Italian-American family which did not focus on "fitness," used food to celebrate life, and valued good performance in school and compliance with the rules. By the time I was 13 years old, I weighed 187 at 5 feet 3 inches. The women on both sides of the family were all overweight, and as a result, my size was not of concern. When I was that age, our family moved to the new culture of Southern California with its outdoor life, and I rapidly became aware of how fat I was. My mother, sympathetic to my plight, talked my Dad into letting me see a doctor who promptly put me on "diet pills," which in the 1950s were amphetamines. I lost 60 pounds with the pills and an eating plan. This was the beginning of a struggle that was to last all my life.

My self-worth and self-esteem became attached to how much I weighed. I married and had three children. Wanting to re-enter the teaching field, I joined Weight Watchers and lost the 60-plus pounds I had regained. I started teaching again, and soon I was a single mother. The next attack on my image came when I started dating again. I was a 40-year-old who found herself competing with young, slim women who seemed to have it all. My weight started to creep up again, and this time I resolved it was to be the last struggle. I joined a health weight-loss program and took off 50 pounds.

That was in 1982, and I have managed, through daily discipline, to keep it off. I have finally made a reasonable peace with my body. I eat well, exercise daily, and try to maintain the attitude that doing this is not temporary. It is a means to keep in place those things I value: my family, my health, and my work. My body is merely the exterior cover of my heart and soul which really give me my value. It's not always easy because women are daily besieged with the image of "perfection." I have not so much wanted to be perfect as to just not have to worry about what I look like. Age has given me some freedom to put aside some of that concern, but now it's become a matter of health—which is a much better reason than perfection.

• *Patty, 64* •

I started my first diet when I was 7 years old, and I've been on a diet since then. Even though, looking back at pictures, I don't know what the big fuss was about, now, at 29, I'm over 300 pounds, and learning to accept myself. I despise the fact that I was taught (by society? family? who knows??) to hate myself and hate my body. Now when I look at my body, I don't see the stretch marks across my belly, or the saggy boobs, I see a round full body, that still isn't "so bad". Of course, other times I look at myself and cringe, wondering still how I "let myself get to this size". I would say that 70 percent of my life has been spent worrying about how I look and how much I weigh. Sad to say, isn't it?

I wonder sometimes if my self-image has held me back in life. I know that it was one of the reasons that I didn't finish college, there was too much fat-hate for me to live there! I also wonder about my profession; as a nurse, people are glad to see me no matter my size (usually). I've always felt in my heart that I'd be a better teacher though, but I know at my size I'd be harassed by the kids constantly. Plus, could I fit in at school...figuratively and literally.

So I guess my body does hold me back in some ways. It's a hard road to accepting myself, and I try to take it a day at a time. At least I've quit fighting myself.

• *Terri, 29* •

Sometimes I think we inherit our ideas about our bodies from our mothers. My mother often had told me that she went on a lifelong diet after she had me. She was always going to a "diet doctor" who would give her pills to pop that zipped her up so much, she would come home from his office and furiously clean the house from top to bottom in less than 20 minutes. She was forever talking through clenched teeth.

She took me for my first visit when I was only 12. I took diet pills throughout my teen years and beyond until they became illegal. The pills helped me lose the weight temporarily, but whenever I looked in the mirror, I was never thin enough and it seemed the only time I got any recognition in my family was when I had managed to lose weight. Of course, the weight never stayed off—especially when I ran out of the pills—and just as my weight seesawed throughout my life, so did my feelings of self-esteem and self-worth.

No matter how much I weighed, it was never good enough for me or for those that I chose to love me, and whenever I looked into the mirror, I would see through emotional eyes and not see the true image reflected. Whatever society dictates as the shape of the day is what is expected of us as women. When I first married in 1966, women were expected to be ornaments to their husbands and I managed to rebel by putting on 30 pounds in the first 6 months. Boy, did I show him! That marriage lasted 2 years.

I always seem to lose the most weight when not in a relationship and so, got thin again, got married again, regained vast amounts of pounds and divorced again. Is there a pattern here? I remember being on a liquid protein diet for 18 months because I was lonely and believed that if I could only get thin enough, I could find someone to love me. All I did was get thin; it took years later to find someone to love me and whom I could love, and that was when I was at my highest weight.

It seems most of my weight always comes to my hips and thighs, areas I have forever hated and judged in myself. About 1984, I was diagnosed with osteoarthritis in my hips and had my first total hip replacement in 1992. It left me with a huge lump on the side of my right thigh, a result of..ugh..even hate to mention it...redistributed body fat! A fluke that happens sometimes with surgery like that.

I had my other hip replaced just this past September. Sometimes I think that maybe my hips died from me not loving them enough. Maybe G-d provided the lesson of learning to love and embrace my whole self through what happened to my hips. I am committed now to learning to love and accept my body/my

46

self as I am. It's been a wonderful vehicle that has carried me to where I now stand in my life. I am truly grateful for the extra padding on my hips that I carry and once despised. It will serve as protection to my new bionic parts against any hurt from falling. I realize how sinful I have been in not loving myself as I know G-d loves me. I have put myself above G-d in thinking, because of my body image, that who I am is so flawed that I'm not worthy of love. I believe in a perfect G-d that only creates perfection; therefore, in all its shapes and forms, in all its flowing changes throughout my life, G-d has manifested perfection in me, in my body, in all of us, just waiting to be discovered.

• *Linda, 54* •

I grew up in a home where my mother was very abusive, both physically and verbally. She was constantly dieting and berating my own appearance. I remember being abandoned in dressing rooms at the age of 5 because I was "too fat" and she was ashamed of me. I was a thin child who was very active and very quiet.

In fifth grade I began to diet. By seventh grade I would skip all my meals except for dinner, and by eighth grade (age 13) I had full-blown anorexia. My weight went up and down as doctors, psychologists, and dieticians monitored me throughout high school. By the time I was 21, my body and mind were a mess. No treatment had helped. I had been hospitalized for suicide attempts and depression. I had a pacemaker from lack of nutrition. I was a wreck.

At 75 pounds and 5 feet 3 and a half inches, I decided to go to Remuda Ranch in Wickenburg, Arizona, where I sit now after four months of treatment. I still continue to struggle, although I have more hope. God is on my side, and I am confident that he is going to help me get through this.

Why do we do this? Why is society so based upon cramming beautiful women into tiny bodies in order to judge us and control us? It's like we are being forced to disappear in either size or importance. It makes me sick. We do not deserve this.

• *Kristin, 21* •

In my family, beauty was an intensely important state of being. I was a beautiful child among beautiful 'children and was praised as such until I approached puberty. By the age of 11, though I still possessed a pretty face, I had developed fully rounded hips, a tiny waist...and huge breasts.

My father, already disappointed in me because of my outspoken responses to his medieval opinions about wives and children (chattel, he called us), began to deride me every evening at the dinner table, calling me a "fat horse" when he observed my well-cleaned plate.

Humiliated at home, I developed feelings of inferiority that have followed me, unreasonably, all my life. I always saw myself as hopelessly fat and lumpy and have fought the battle of the bulge my whole life, never being content with my body.

I married at 17, weighing 165 pounds. Over the years, my weight has bounced between 135 and 180 depending on how frustrated I have been, my level of activity, my resolve to diet, etc. Though I grew into a very attractive woman, I was haunted by the way men looked at me, the attitudes they expressed about me that had nothing to do with who I was, what I thought or knew.

I was married and divorced three times, and part of the reason for that was that I could never really feel loved in spite of what my husbands said. I didn't love me so how could anyone else?

• *Geri, 65* •

My story is nothing dramatic. I haven't got any real "clincher" endings, or incredible sayings. My problems with my body image came insidiously. Slowly, repeatedly, seemingly forever. Now, my negative feelings about my body are invisible because they're buried so deep.

When I was about 5, I was thinking that I would make a pretty good Mouseketeer. I could sing, I could act, I thought I was cute. What did that girl, Karen, have that I didn't have? I started doing little skits around the house. My older sister laughed at me. My mom told me to settle down and not to be so vain. "Those kids on TV are special." Blam!

I was 6 or 7 when my "big teeth" came in. Boy were they BIG. Real big. My sisters and my cousin thought it was pretty funny to call me "Bucky Beaver." When I cried, my mom told me to grow up.

And I did grow up. I went on my first diet and lost eight pounds when I was 12, trying to fit into the Twiggy mode. At 13, they gave me a new nickname, "Mick Jagger," because my lips are "full."

My older sister was studying *Pride and Prejudice* in English class. The heroine kept a "hope chest" in expectation of marriage. One character said, "My sisters will never marry. They have no hope." My sister took one look at my tiny, budding breasts and declared that I had a "hopeless" chest. Another body part shot to hell.

I can't pick a single incident, or anecdote and say, "That's the one. That's the time that my self-esteem ran away and never came back." For me, it was hundreds of little things, year after year.

The only relief I think I've ever had is now that I'm over 40, and overweight. Now, when I walk into a room, or down the street, or go to the beach, I don't have to worry about my looks. I'm a middle-aged mother of two who's out of shape. What I look like doesn't matter. To the average onlooker, I don't exist.

• *Ann, 47* •

At age 12, I began to look like my Irish grandmother's family: round and very bosomy. My mother and doctor, alarmed at my "over-development," put me on diet pills. Between that and the usual social pressure to be thin, I spent the next 25 years dieting (and, of course, gaining it all back—with additions).

I wore clothes designed to conceal my shape. But even at my thinnest, I still wore a 36DD, and I considered breast reduction surgery for a long time. Finally, in my late thirties, I found a photo of myself at age 12, and realized that I'd been the victim of other people's ideas of how a 12-year-old girl "should" look. I swore off dieting forever.

Since then, I've been a backpacker and a hiker, I dress as I please, and I've recently taken up belly dancing. I'm healthier (mentally and physically) than I ever was in my dieting days. But the number of people who accuse me of being "unfit" is still appalling ... we've got a long way to go!

• *Paula, 54* •

Body image is a funny thing for women: None of us see ourselves as we really are. Maybe we look in the mirror and see the person we once were, or maybe we look in the mirror and see our mothers, or maybe we see an entirely distorted image we've created in our heads. But I think we rarely see ourselves as we really are. The scary thing is that sometimes we do not even see others as they really are.

My mother had a profound influence on how I look at food and weight and my body. When I was growing up, she was gaining weight. I do not ever remember her going on a diet, but I remember her terror that I would grow fat. I would never find a husband, she said, if I was fat. I could never be pretty, she said, if I was fat. Now, mind you, I was underweight, perhaps seriously underweight, at this point, but she was terrified I would get fat. At mealtime my mother would serve the food and decide on portions. I remember always being hungry, and if I complained, my mother would tell me she was doing me a favor, that she didn't want me to get fat.

The only time I wasn't hungry was at Thanksgiving or Christmas or Halloween. The situation was so extreme that my freshman year of college (when I could eat as much as I wanted in the dorm cafeteria) I grew two inches in height and gained 20 pounds, and I still looked too thin!

It took me years to stop being afraid of food, to let myself eat if I was hungry—instead of on a rigid schedule. It took years for me to be able to eat in front of other people. It took even longer to let myself enjoy food instead of seeing it as a potential enemy. There was a time when I was 5 feet 10 inches and weighed 110 pounds. I didn't want to be that thin, but I hadn't learned yet how to eat or enjoy eating.

What appalls me is how many people, including some doctors, would tell me at the time how good I looked, how great it was that I was so thin! I knew it wasn't healthy, and I couldn't understand how they could think it was. Eventually I threw out my scale because it wasn't helping me gain weight anyway. I decided to eat healthy and not worry about whether I would gain weight or not. And I began to choose clothes I loved rather than clothes that would make me look the way I thought I ought to look.

Now my weight is stable and healthy and I like who I am when I look in the mirror. But I cringe when I look at models in magazines who are waif-thin. I know how cold I was when I was underweight, I know how often I got sick or felt so very tired. I want to take them and feed them a good meal and tell them to just enjoy life rather than worrying about how they look!

I am a writer, and in my latest novel I purposely made the heroine a big woman—a big woman whose mother had always wanted a "dainty Juliet" for a daughter. And part of Juliet's journey in the book is coming to terms with who she is and finding someone who loves her as she is.

Our culture says that thin is beautiful, that this is how to attract a man, but the one woman I know who is always surrounded by men at parties is a big woman. She is, by any medical standards, overweight; but she loves life and she loves men (though she is happily married and faithful) and that draws men to her faster than anyone else I have ever seen. I would hope that we could all, whatever our body shapes, have her *joie de vivre* ! That, to me, is real beauty.

• April, 48 •

In 1967, when I was nearly 40, the deaths of my parents released me from failing to measure up. Dad had wanted a boy, but as their only child, I was only a tomboy. Throughout my childhood I was muscular and husky, athletic and strong. Dad had persuaded me that playing ball meant throwing harder, straighter, and farther than any boy we knew. At age 11, all that changed.

My swelling breasts and spreading hips forced Dad into relinquishing his desire that I develop height and wide shoulders while I also slimmed down at the hips. Although menarche released us both from any question about my being female, it did not release me from my given name.

"Diane reflects the goddess of the chase," Dad said. "By ancient silver moonlight, Diane hunts the deer. She is slender and willowy, long-limbed and pale-skinned, graceful, swift, and soft-voiced."

I fit none of these physical traits, either before or after my first-blood. My Mum was far closer than I to mirroring the Huntress of the Forest. She was the very essence of ladylike—well-groomed, well-coifed, and well-spoken, the last meaning quiet. I remember Mum scolding me to be ladylike and to lower my voice. "People can hear you 40 miles away in a roaring hurricane."

My parents' deaths released me from 40 years of trying to measure up, and of missing the mark. Their deaths also emptied me out. My grief felt more like renunciation than sorrow, but who let whom fade away was not at all clear. I searched for something to refill the zero-place left by their deaths. For 20 years, until 1987, I fed being empty with empty calories. I laughed at and decried the advertisements promising youth-like female beauty to women my age (read: postmenopausal), and I indulged my appetite for thick historical novels and old photograph albums.

It was the albums that filled me up. Finally, gradually, over a 20-year period, I found refuge in my own bloodlines. I saw myself as the product of anomalous genes. Dad inherited his mother's Celtic traits, not the male Saxon ones for light-colored hair and wiry strength. Mum was both short and thin in a family whose members were either tall and lean or short and stocky.

Both my grandmothers were sturdy, like thumbs of squat rock jutting out of the sea's edge. Their mothers were round (spherical), resonant of voice (loud), rooted yet awkward of movement (wild), swarthy of face, full-breasted, and big-bellied. You've seen my like today in the valleys of Wales, the glens of Strathclyde, and on museum shelves where small stone statues carved by prehistoric artists tell you who I am.

I am an earthmother, sturdy as a thumb and solid as a rock. My eyes are light in color—tawny and flecked with copper. I am the goddess of the golden eye, and a wise old owl.

• Dianne, 70 •

I am 10 years old when my parents split up for the first time. Soon after my father left, I hear my mother call me into my bedroom with rage smoldering in her voice. "Crumbs! In your bed! How could crumbs get into your bed? Did you sneak food into your bed?"

I do not say anything. I am afraid of her, despite the fact that she is 5 feet and weighs about 100 pounds. I am scared of her because she is my mother, left by my father, and is looking like she wants to kill me.

"Who put the crumbs in your bed?"

"I don't know," I mutter.

"Oh, I-don't-know-did-it! I-don't-know-put the crumbs in your bed!"

Her sarcastic Brooklyn tone shames me. I am a bad girl. There is something wrong with me. I can't control my little-girl hungers, and I got caught.

"Well," she gasps with tears in her eyes, "let's get I-don't-know in here and have him clean the crumbs out of your bed!" And with that, she runs into her own room, throws her petite body on her own empty bed and weeps for hours while I try not to listen.

I've failed her again. I've hurt my mom again. She is miserable because I hid four pieces of Wonderbread in the elastic of my panties and snuck them into my room so I could feel the goodness, without getting yelled at because I eat too much. I like it under my covers, when no one is watching me and I can calm myself with cookies and Wonderbread. Under my covers, no one can look at me and say, "You don't want to eat that!"

Those people always make me laugh inside. The people who say, "You don't want to eat that!" I never have the courage to wheel around and say to them, "No, YOU don't want to eat that. Because you don't think of food as your hero. As your savior. As tender as Jesus. As evil as Satan. As confusing as all the religions and philosophies of the world. Food is my secret poet. My armless lover. And yes, I do want to eat that. I want to eat everything. I feel as if I could eat everything and never get full. Never. For everything is as big as the hole inside of me."

Now I'm grown, and my adorable mother no longer yells at me about food, Wonderbread, or crumbs in my bed. She stays away from the topic completely. She has given up. But her voice has never left. It has metamorphosed into The Giant's voice. The Giant lives inside of me now. The Giant yells at me for eating too much, smoking too much, not going to the gym enough, gaining a pound,

56

not being like the thin girls who know they must stay thin and attractive if they are to seduce a man.

She, The Giant, calls me a loser. I cannot seduce a man. Repel, maybe, but not seduce. I live under the weight of her. She, The Giant, is hundreds of pounds heavier than my own body could ever be. My therapist says I have negative voices in my head and must learn to hear new voices, benevolent voices, positive voices. But I don't know from where. As I look down on my thighs and belly, I do not know where these kind voices will come from since The Giant takes up most of the space in my head. I am pretty. But I am fat. I am sexy. But I am fat. I am talented. But I am fat. I am hiding-slovenly-lazy-apathetic-lonely and isolated because I am fat.

When The Giant is sleeping, I know that I am lovely, sweet, sexy. I know how deeply I can love, how deeply I can become involved. I know my passions and my desires when The Giant is asleep. And these days I try to let a benevolent voice slip in. It is a small voice. A little voice that I can barely hear. I don't like to speak of it, for The Giant may hear and become jealous. She would wipe the tiny voice away. So tiny it brushes against me like the belly of a kitten. So soft, the voice says, "It's okay. You're okay. You are doing good. You only have this short amount of time here. Don't live for your future—the future in which you are thin and loved. Live now, love. Live in the present, where you are yourself and are loved. If you could take me in, I could help nourish you. I love you." And then she fades away.

I am left with her missive. And The Giant sleeps. And I am left alone. I breathe in a bit of freedom and swallow it.

• *Shawn, 37* •

I Am the Same Person

I have put on 40 pounds in the past 10 years, and in the eyes of the world I have apparently disappeared. That sounds like a contradiction. After all, what are the fat and the flesh hanging onto? The physical woman is very much there in her size 16 and Elizabeth size 1 clothing. She is still there in her lack of a waist and her tops and jackets, worn long to cover her butt. She is very much there when she notices that the airplane seats seem a little snugger than they used to. What a shock it is to me to feel that because of a weight gain, in the eyes of friends, I seem to have become a different person.

Ten years ago I had a hysterectomy. It was one of the best things I ever did because I flooded so badly every month. Although I kept my ovaries, it was the beginning of menopause. I began slowly to gain weight, and the older I got the more I gained. I still ate properly and exercised, but it was as if my body had a mind and a shape of its own. It was as if I had returned to my teenage years when I had no control over the shape my body was taking.

I think that because I developed so early—I looked like a 16-year-old when I was only 12—that I thought I was fat. I inherited my breasts from my mother's family, and they were way too big for my age. So began the vision in my head of never being thin when in fact I had a normal-sized body.

Now I do not think of myself as fat, but when I see pictures I am shocked. And nobody ever tells me that I look good anymore, or that my outfit is stunning. I turn on my smile and pretend that I look like the same person that I have always been!

• Ann, 47 •

You take off your clothes and in the full-length mirror inspect red creases cut into your flesh by your minimizer bra and elastic-waist pants. Quickly, you pull on an oversized bathrobe. You were a walk-around-naked kind of gal until recently, at least when nobody else was around. Now, you feel ashamed even when you're home alone.

Your boyfriend is horny and full of flattery. He claims to be turned on by your curves and rolls but you know he harbors fantasies of his ex-girlfriend. In fact, he dreams of her flat belly and small breasts, her pre-pubescent figure.

You know this because you read his diary.

You had been looking for some paper to write a letter, and after searching your own desk drawers for clean notebooks, you decided to check his, telling yourself there might be one but also knowing the bottom left drawer mostly holds old journals. You opened a steno notebook with a smooth, unbent cover and only a few used pages, the first of which contained an ode to the legs of teenaged girls. At the bottom of the page you saw your own name, so of course felt justified to read on, only to discover, with a roiling in your gut, that he was comparing your looks, unfavorably, to those of his last girlfriend, with whom he broke up many months before you met.

"How is it that I want to fuck Z, and still come home to X?" he wrote. He detailed his sexual fantasies about her; he waxed poetic about her body. You, he called "sweet."

You taste puke.

The rational part of your mind knows you came out ahead in his appraisal, kind of. Still, you want to throw up your last seven meals, stick toothpicks in his and his ex's eyes, and perhaps devour an entire box of Fudgesicles, not necessarily in that order. For months and months, you will wonder if he's fantasizing about this other woman every time he's in bed with you. You will snoop in his date book, convinced he's secretly meeting with her. You will study snapshots of her, them, in his photo album. You will drop increasingly bolder hints, wondering aloud about their relationship, their breakup ("Whose idea was it, anyway?"), does he still think about her—all but actually admit to snooping. You will even consider calling her number. In fact, you may actually dial it once, but of course you will hang up before anyone answers. Later you will fret about caller ID.

In couples' therapy, months later, you will confess, just to the snooping. By then he will have hurt you so deeply, in so many ways, that you will feel morally superior and not at all repentant. Your therapist, a woman, will pretend to be objective, but in the car on the way home, you will agree that she takes your side.

Although you will tuck it into a rarely visited part of your brain, even after you find someone better, and even after you buff up to the point of wearing snug-fitting t-shirts and consider revealing your navel—in public—you will never forget what he wrote. That's what you get for snooping.

• *Lisa, 30* •

At the Health Club

Okay, I manage the bad news.
Okay, I manage the mastectomy.
How will I manage swim suits?
I find out how. Okay.
How do I manage the locker room?
Being naked in the hot tub?
Not okay.
No one wants to be reminded
Of disease at the health club.
I'm still me, but now an amputee.
Not okay.
Schooled in not offending all my life,
I keep to myself,
Change clothes in a corner,
Wear a swimsuit in the hot tub.
The disease is common.
Not okay.
Where are the rest of
The one-breasted women?
I wonder.

• *Sheila, 57* •

My earliest memories are of a healthy, chubby-faced little girl with ringlets and smiling cheeks that hid her eyes. In grade school, I was 5 feet tall, taller than the boys, heavier than most of the girls, but I rode my bike and walked daily. I was strong and healthy.

When I reached puberty, things began to shift. My round tummy dropped to my hips. Ripe breasts blossomed, and boys became quite interested in my developing curves. By high school I was 5 feet 6 inches tall, 130 pounds, and filled out my jeans rather well. Many of my friends were still straight in the hip and barely budding on top, so as usual I felt large and cumbersome.

Twiggy was the role model we all strived to be, and I couldn't possibly squeeze even my foot into size 2 hip-huggers. When my Dad remarried, I was bigger than my new stepsister who was petite at 5 feet 2 inches, 89 pounds. I was 2 inches taller and 10 pounds heavier than my stepmother as well. They gave me the nickname "Chunky," like the candy bar, and teased me about my roundness. I became obsessed with losing weight, and for the next 30 years of my life, I've tried one diet after another. I've joined Weight Watchers (three times), Diet Center (once), and tried any new fad diet to come along.

The grapefruit diet made my teeth ache. The banana diet gave me gas. The protein diet caused constipation, and the high-fiber diet gave me the runs. I've counted points, calories, fat grams, weighed, measured, and altered recipes. When I met my husband, I was living on my own and very thin. I couldn't afford to eat much. When we got married and we had two incomes, we had a full pantry. I loved cooking and trying new recipes. We both gained 20 pounds the first month of marital bliss.

When I had my son, I gained 40 pounds and only lost 20 after he was born. I recall being called a beached whale as I lay on the floor, eight months pregnant, doing my Lamaze exercises. When I changed from a sales job to a desk job, I started spreading immediately. In an effort to combat the advance, I enthusiastically joined Jazzercise and hurt my back. After weeks of chiropractic treatments, I tried water aerobics. The chlorine fried my hair and ate the elastic in my bleached-out black swimsuit.

That's when I decided it was time to improve my mind and go back to college in the evenings. For the past five years I've been working full time and attending classes at night. I've developed tendonitis in my writing arm and fibromyalgia in my joints. I have also blossomed to a full-figured woman who's fast approaching 200 pounds.

My husband has made beeping sounds when I back up, and comments on my clothes not fitting well. The joke about me not fitting through the attic entry, however, hurt, especially coming from my mother-in-law. It would seem that no matter how much I am loved, my appearance is not. I'm one of those women that "has such a pretty face." Not only do I have a pretty face, but I have a strong body that takes care of me, an active mind that stimulates me, and a creative and loving spirit that sustains me and those around me.

It is sad that those that I love cannot see past the body to the shining essence that is me. If I had the time, money, and support, I would exercise more, cook more healthy, and probably lose some weight. But it angers me that it matters so much to others, and interferes with how I view myself.

I am glad that I didn't have to watch a daughter grow up in this society that values appearance above a caring and loving heart. But if I had, maybe I could have helped her realize how beautiful we can be, no matter what size.

• *Bonnie, 44* •

My size and shape developed when I was about 8. That's when I got my first "chubby" dress, and when I first knew I was different from and less than other girls. I remember sitting all alone on the steps of the cafeteria crying because I thought no one liked me or ever would. I spent many years trying to be better than everyone else at whatever I could—grades, art, whatever—because I knew I started out less than.

In high school, I was teased to such an extent that I was convinced I was less than human, and certainly not a woman. Women were thin. I was fat, and no one would ever love me so I might as well get used to it. I fell in love many times, but never expected it to be returned. How could anyone love me? I starved myself and got thin, but it was too late, the fat girl inside would never be convinced she was worthy of love or success or power or sex or anything at all she wanted.

As I went through my twenties, I tried to accept myself, to love myself, to care for myself. I still thought if I did that, I would get thin and be loved. Someday I would be worthy of everything I wanted, would be entitled to everything I am. I made great strides. I fell in love with someone who loved me, even though I was not as thin as I should be. I am fatter now, and somehow he still loves me. We've been together eight years. Wow. I am thinking now and feeling like people I know who were gay as long as they've been alive and finally admitted it to the world. Hey, I'm fat!

I'm a large woman, and I'm tired of pretending I'm not. I want to stop trying to "pass." I want to eat what I want, care for my body the way it wants. I want to be a person with the same right to sexuality and art and success and power as anyone else. I'm not better because I'm fat, I just don't want to be nobody. I want to be large in spirit and heart. I'm so weary of trying to be small.

• *Kathleen, 40* •

All through my adolescence and young adulthood I was thin. I took the sexual attention that I got from it for granted. I thought that since I disliked sweets I would never get fat. I had a run-in with heroin addiction at 25 and then got on methadone, a medication that saved my life but took its payment for doing so by causing me to gain over 100 pounds. Now everyone treats me differently.

I can feel their response to seeing my body: it is revulsion. It is anger at having to look at me! That's how conditioned they are—they are literally angry at me for being what they consider an eyesore because of my belly. The men want big bumps on the top of a woman's chest but a big bump half a foot lower is anathema. Go figure. (No pun intended... .)

Currently I have a boyfriend who lives with me, who loves my mind so much it seems my body does not bother him. He never watches television and knows full well that ads are computer enhanced. Thank the Forces That Be that at least one person does not take the lie to heart, but takes the truth: the truth of "me."

And yet, I still would literally give my right arm to be rid of that 100 pounds.

• *Demi, 34* •

The most humiliating experience I ever had occurred one day while I was shopping. A young mother and her two children, aged about 3 and 6, came upon me in the aisle. The 6-year-old boy told his mother, "That lady is overweight." He kept saying it over and over. I wanted to go up to the mother and ask her what other prejudices she was instilling in her children, but I didn't. I just finished my shopping and went home feeling miserable.

The standard for beauty today, as seen in movies, TV, and magazines, is impossible to achieve without "enhancement surgery." A long, lanky-boned body usually comes with small breasts. So larger breasts have to be installed. I recently turned on the TV and caught a bit of a daytime trash show, where women were revealing if their breasts were real or fake. The skinny ones all had fake ones, of course, but they got cheers. The ones with big boobs that were real, were all full-figured as well, and were reviled by the audience. There is our culture's take on beauty today!

• *Judy, 53* •

I am a tiny girl, about 5 feet 7 inches, and I weigh only about 103 pounds. I hate to hear that stuff about thin women because I have always been so tiny! I have hated it, have had to hear "You're so skinny" all my life! I even have a 6-year-old son, and I'm still thin.

I always thought I was never enough compared to all the girls with shapes and big boobies. People are always asking if I eat or if I am anorexic. Its just like saying "Man, you're SO FAT!" It hurts just as bad!

Women are so cruel, they always want to make me think I'm odd. I've been pointed at and had people tell stories on me. I've heard "Do you do drugs?" and that's even worse! I've cried myself to sleep many nights wishing I could be bigger! So when you see a skinny girl and you get mad at her, STOP! Don't tell her she's different. Maybe you'll hurt her! I don't have a problem at all. I eat whatever I want, and all day I eat and eat! I just don't gain any weight.

I have decided to accept my shape. I started modeling. I still feel inadequate at times and want a boob job or a few extra pounds, but mostly I will thank God for my self, my good heart, my acceptance of others' differences, and my son! So when you think of the little people, we are just like the ones who are over-weight and have been ridiculed. Don't judge a book by its cover. I have A BIG HEART!!

• *Cassandra, 25* •

A CIRCLE WITHIN A CIRCLE

We posted an invitation on one of Ms. Magazine's bulletin boards (www.msmagazine.com), for women to engage in an on-line dialogue on the subject of body image and beauty. The cyber conversations that ensued are compelling and intimate illustrations of women's struggles, strengths and support of one another. We are including them here as a circle within a circle.

I do not believe that new stories will find their way into texts if they do not begin in oral exchange among women in groups hearing and talking to one another.

• Carolyn Heilbrun •

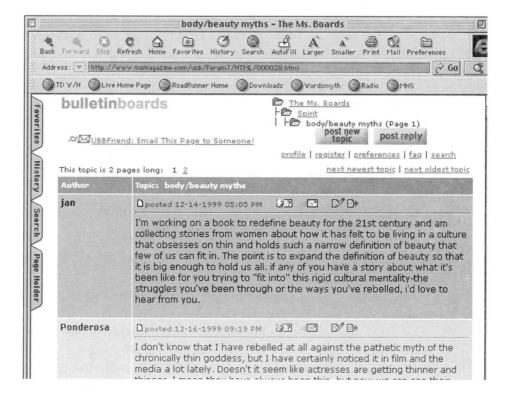

A Cyber Conversation on Body/Beauty Myths • Posted 12-14-1999 • 05:05 PM

jan   posted 12-14-1999 05:05 PM

I'm working on a book to redefine beauty for the 21st century and am collecting stories from women about how it has felt to be living in a culture that obsesses on thin and holds such a narrow definition of beauty that few of us can fit in. The point is to expand the definition of beauty so that it is big enough to hold us all. If any of you have a story about what it's been like for you trying to "fit into" this rigid cultural mentality—the struggles you've been through or the ways you've rebelled, I'd love to hear from you.

Ponderosa   posted 12-16-1999 09:19 PM

I don't know that I have rebelled at all against the pathetic myth of the chronically thin goddess, but I have certainly noticed it in film and the media a lot lately. Doesn't it seem like actresses are getting thinner and thinner? I mean they have always been thin, but now we can see their ribs just below the collar bone. What, do they think they're fooling anyone? We all know that is not natural.

lizzie   posted 12-17-1999 02:54 AM

I read an article (in *Glamour*, I'm ashamed to admit) about an actress (Kathy Griffin) who had liposuction to come down from a size FOUR! She had a disastrous experience, but I just can't believe that the ideal now is a size 2 or 1 or 0, that's just disgusting, that's GAUNT! It seems like if we're going to have an unrealistic beauty ideal it could at least be ATTRACTIVE!

Shan   posted 12-17-1999 09:38 AM

I don't think that beauty should extend to the selfish or the willfully ignorant, the mean-spirited or the narrow-minded or the shallow or the unrelentingly vain. On the same note, but less condemnatory, I don't think that beauty should ex-tend to people who have bought in to the beauty myth to the point that it ruins their lives. They have an illness; our culture should identify and help this, not romanticize the effects of the illness (this is not to say that genuinely thin people need to be demonized. It does not mean that people with eating disorders need to be demonized, either; but anorexia needs to stop being considered rather lovely, really, by the mainstream).

Beauty needs to be redefined to take in everybody who tries to be decent and kind and involved with others and intellectually active and proud of their bodies and their interactions with the world.

To me, the fact that any doctor would AGREE to give a size four human being LIPO is DISGUSTING. It shouldn't be LEGAL! It was the first "aesthetic, cosmetic surgery with a mortality rate" according to the article!

Shan, I was anorexic for three years and got the most compliments at my worst—102 pounds at 5 feet 8. I could literally feel myself in danger of floating away sometimes; I was sick, hungry, constantly freezing, fragile, achy, incoherent...and people were telling me I looked great. And I believed them over my friends and family who were telling me I looked horrible. I was a size 1 or 2, but my mind and spirit had shrunk out of existence; that this is what young girls are taught to strive for is unconscionable.

However, I think a large part of the myth of thinness has to do with something few people ever acknowledge: REAL models are aberrations. My friend works in the fashion industry and I remember her telling me when she was an intern that the models were so scary-looking, they looked disproportionate and awkward—6 feet 2 inches and 110 or 120 isn't what we would define as typically "PRETTY" up close and in person—in magazines and on runways, as hangers for clothes, their bodies are long and lean enough to be used effectively and flatteringly, but they are NOT the norm, and somehow our culture has adopted their image as just that!

I did not look glamorous when I fit the Hollywood ideal of size 1. My hair was dry and brittle, my skin was yellow, my clothes hung off me like I was a little kid playing dress-up. Size 1 is fine if you were born that way (I have a cousin who is 5 feet and 90 pounds and she'll simply never, ever be heavy, but she is healthy as a horse); but so are sizes 8 and 10 and 16. Even as I say it, however, I know it's harder than just having that knowledge and believing it, because I'm still recovering from anorexia; I still succumb to the mind-fuck once in a while, sometimes I want that size 1 body back, can't stand taking up space, feeling the weight of my own body around me...but it can be done! We all really need to be conscious of it and make other women and girls conscious too...

Fire   ☐ posted 12-17-1999 05:56 PM   [icons]

I am 5 feet 1 and three-quarters inches and weigh 121 pounds; I haven't grown since eighth grade. My little sister is 5 feet 9, weighs about 98 pounds, and has always picked on me for being "fat." Needless to say, it has taken several loving people to help me re-establish my "vision" of myself. I now know that emaciatedly thin is not what the majority of people want in their everyday lives; there's nothing to hold on to. I now love my hourglass figure and wouldn't trade it for the world. I can fill out my clothes, they don't just hang on me. And I've actually taken a poll among my friends and associates. The majority of the men and lesbians polled did find a fuller female figure more sexually attractive, and it also makes them feel more comfortable.

Shan   ☐ posted 12-17-1999 08:07 PM   [icons]

I was bulimic something like ten years ago (I guess I still am, but am "recovering"). I lost 50 pounds in six months, and to this day I feel guilty because I still believe that that was the phase of my life in which I was the most "beautiful." It's crap, of course. I was passing out all over the place; I was shamed, and my breath stank. But the reinforcement was there. People were telling me that I looked great, even people who should have known better. And I know that there are few things harder than getting past this. I'm still not entirely there. I have decided to call myself voluptuous and be done with it, and I have the immense advantage of a partner who loves me, who knew me back then, who finds me sexier now, and this really helps. Naked, I feel great. But socially, well, it's another matter.
Please, know that you are beautiful.

Janine   ☐ posted 12-18-1999 04:09 AM   [icons]

First off, been close to where you were, though not quite as bad, and so was my mother, so I'm sending out my congratulations to you emcd, fire, Shan . The greatest compliment I ever got was from a guy who told me that although

I'm far from the cover girl/porn star ideal, I have a lust for life that's really sexy. Because that's what it comes down to, doesn't it? You want to be sexy. But "sexy" and "thin" or even "pretty" are not always synonyms. "Sexy" and "confident" are.

JeanC    posted 12-19-1999 01:08 AM

I've been quietly active in the fat/size/acceptance movement since I finally decided to get off the diet-go-round and accept that I was a big woman and was always going to be a big woman. I kept trying to diet myself down to the "acceptable" 105 pounds I was told I should be at 5 feet 3, even though looking at pics of my grandmothers, great-grandmothers and other female relatives showed I was genetically programmed to be 150-160 pounds. I come from good, hardy, Highland stock and was never going to be a waif. I tried practically everything, though I never did let my self get sucked into the "Jenny Craig-Nutri System-(name the franchise of the week)." I did do Cambridge (lost a bit of weight on the 330 calories a day, but when I dropped the one shake and added the "sensible" 500 calorie meal I regained all I lost and then some (even though I was still eating less than 1100 calories a day). I tried the over-the-counter diet pills, and almost died one night when my heart did things it wasn't supposed to do without a cardiac crash cart handy.

Funny thing, when I stopped dieting, I stopped gaining weight, no matter what I ate. I was healthy, active, and my blood sugars, cholesterol, and blood pressure have always been normal or low. I drove my doctors nuts because at 250 pounds they kept saying I should not be as healthy as I was. In fact, the only major health problem I have has nothing to do with my weight! I have been lucky recently to have found a doctor who knows diets don't work, tend to cause more harm than good, and would prefer his patients to keep stable weights, eat healthy, and get good exercise.

I have found a lot of good reading material in my search for self-acceptance. If anyone is interested in that kind of reading, I have a list on my website at http://www.uidaho.edu/~bjcraw/books.htm

"To lose confidence in one's body is to lose confidence in oneself."

• *Simone de Beauvoir* •

▯ posted 12-26-1999 11:48 PM

I'm sort of doing the "diet-go-round" now myself. I'm recovering from anorexia (yuck, I hate that word), but I still think about food all the time, count calories, and feel fat sometimes. I wish I could just go back to being a little kid, before I knew that eating could make you fat (or not eating could make you thin!), and just enjoy myself, and get myself out of this trap in which I think about my next meal constantly. I'm so disgusted with myself. Feminism has helped me a lot, but I still can't seem to reprogram my mind to stop thinking about food.

emcd ▯ posted 12-27-1999 12:22 AM

I was anorexic for about 3 and a half years, and I still have disordered eating habits because, as you said, I can't seem to "reprogram" my brain. Once you've thought about food as consistently and compulsively as you do when you're anorexic, it's just not possible to recover in a day or a week or even 2 or 3 years. It's a really gradual process that will get better with time, but maybe never go completely away. I still regress every once in a while (holidays are BRUTAL), and I constantly feel fat now that I try to eat more normally, but I have definitely seen an improvement as far as how much I concentrate on food itself. Like you, feminism is the thing that got me thinking.

I was reading *The Beauty Myth* by Naomi Wolf, and it suddenly hit me like a ton of bricks that I was walking around feeling depressed and angry and apathetic about life and hey, maybe it's simply because I'm nutritionally defunct... maybe I feel weak and tired all the time because I am eating almost nothing healthy at all.

I had become so accustomed to my pathetic diet that I had stopped thinking about it as a problem; I had incorporated it into my daily life. I feel so much more clear-headed now and I'm pretty sure I could never go back to starving myself again (my stomach actually growls when it's hungry again, something it had completely unlearned when I was eating rice cakes and frozen glacé for breakfast, lunch, and dinner). All I can tell you, Moondance, is that you sound like you're on the right track and just don't give up! I think about the way I used to view food when I was little, too—I used to eat whole bags of Doritos and pints of chocolate chocolate chip ice cream in one shot without a second thought! Now, if I eat ice cream, it has to be fat free, or if it's low fat I calculate the calories per cup divided by 4 to figure out approximately how many calories and fat are in that one spoonful—it's ridiculous! But at the height of anorexia, my mind was one continuous stream of calorie and fat facts, lists of foods I could eat, diets planned out for the next day; it's hysterical, but I never thought more about food in my life than when I wasn't eating any.

JeanC ☐ posted 12-27-1999 12:34 AM 🔲 🔲 🔲 🔲

Hi Moondance: There are a couple of books on my list that I can recommend to try and deal with issues with food. They are: Bruno, Barbara Altman, Ph.D., *Worth your weight: what you can do about a weight problem*. Rutledge Books, Inc., 1996.
Waterhouse, Debra, MPH, RD. *Like mother, like daughter: how women are influenced by their mothers' relationship with food—and how to break the pattern*. Hyperion, 1997.
There is very good info here, and they have references for other reading.
I think the issues that have been programmed into us by family and society about food is one of the major reasons women have so many problems. How many women's magazines have articles about "losing X pounds" right next to the high-calorie gooey desserts you are supposed to feed your family (but you aren't supposed to eat because it is fattening and you aren't supposed to enjoy yourself anyways because that is selfish and you should be sacrificing yourself for your family?) In the meantime, do you have a support group available? If not, and you are interested in an online support group, there is an eating disorders group at Support-group.com. The URL is: http://www.support-group.com/cgi-bin/sg/get_links?eating_disorders
I find there are a lot of folks who are good to talk to at support-group.com. Take care.

Moondance ☐ posted 12-27-1999 12:05 PM 🔲 🔲 🔲 🔲

Thank you all SO MUCH. When I came back in the morning, it was like a miracle—all these people who cared about me! Emcd, I read *The Beauty Myth* too. Sometimes, while I was reading it, though, I still felt like this was somebody else's problem, and if I wanted to survive in this society, I had to keep molding my body the way people wanted. Now, though, it's not even about my body. It's about my mind. It's as if my body and mind are two totally separate parts of me...my body is so disconnected, you know? Now it's like my mind is just battling my mind, now that my body is technically healthy (even if it's still a little underweight).

I just can't shut up my mind, so how can I make my mind internalize Naomi Wolf's message? I hear it, but it feels like it's distant; it's right, and I should listen, and my conscious- ness is listening, but not that little voice inside me that still wants to plan its meals. I go to Barnes and Noble and read everything they have on the shelves about eating disorders. But, somehow, I missed those books that JeanC suggested. I'm gonna go to the library today and look for those books. I might also check out that online support group. Oh no. My dad's coming in. I don't want him to see this. Thanks every- body!

emcd    posted 12-27-1999 12:46 PM

Yeah, I know what you mean, Moondance—I still find my- self in the bathroom every once in a while contemplating expulsion of everything in my stomach, despite the fact that I am completely and totally aware that it is silly and danger- ous and playing into mainstream media mind-fuck propa- ganda; despite the fact that the larger percentage of my brain doesn't WANT to throw up, thinks it's disgusting and pa- thetic and is so sick of it already....it really is a mind-over- matter situation and lots of times, the "matter" wins out still. Something definitely "snapped" in my head when I chose to become anorexic—it's like this little group of brain cells decided to take over and become the Hitler of my head, and even though I think I've killed him now, it's gonna take a while for all the damage he's done to go away.

Simone    posted 12-28-1999 01:38 AM

I was anorexic for two years in high school and it is so hard to push my unhealthy anorexic-head thoughts away, espe- cially with all those "Lose 10 pounds easy before swimsuit season!" magazine covers staring me in the thighs at every supermarket checkout counter. Moondancer, congratulations on your ongoing recovery. It is a lifelong odyssey, but feminism is a great help. Actually, being anorexic is what helped turn me into a feminist. Like emcd, when I was at my unhealthiest gaunt weight of 80 pounds, everyone encouraged my diseased mindset by saying such helpful things as "I wish I was as skinny as you—you have such great self-control."

It wasn't until I realized I was taking control of my weight because nothing else was in control that I decided to scrap all the conventional non-wisdom about being a good, responsible, dutiful daughter/girlfriend/woman/student and do whatever the heck felt healthy. Although sometimes it is hard to feel healthy when you are eating not because you are hungry but because you know you have to, and while you watch your "delicate" bones slowly become enveloped in "ugly" flesh. I guess you can tell I still have a ways to go, too. I still find myself rationalizing cutting meals or drooling over the liposuction ads in the paper (although since I'm a size 7 and not a size 4, like Kathy Griffin, I am actually in desperate NEED of a lipo, says my little anorexic-head). Maybe my little Hitler faked his bunker suicide and is really hiding out somewhere...

In response to Jan, and the original topic of this board, I think beauty should be measured in confidence, compassion, usefulness and selflessness.

Moondance   posted 12-28-1999 11:55 AM   

Every time I come back to read these boards, I am reminded that there is so much hope. I think that everyone on here who is conscious about the "mind-fuck" being done to them is really healthier in mind than they feel, because a lot of my friends aren't even conscious of the Hitler in their heads that was inserted by this thin-obsessed society, so it's like they're wandering around in a daze, which they are even physically, since their fat free rice cakes certainly aren't giving them enough energy! Anyway, I was thinking, maybe if I convinced some of them to come to these boards...

Wouldn't it be awesome if guys, just for one day, had to be girls? If they had to have those thunderous thoughts pounding in their heads every moment they weren't reading or writing or watching TV? I wish my dad could be a girl for a day. Maybe then he'd stop hounding me, and start to understand the terror of flesh around your bones.

But I've gained some weight, and you know what? So far, it

doesn't feel that bad...I'm just terrified that any moment I'll realize it and panic and want to be thin again. But for now I just won't think about it. But don't you hate it when those size 0 jeans that were once wonderfully baggy around your thighs squeeze you so that you have to move up to a size 1, and you think, "what have I done?" and you keep eating because you know that's what you're supposed to do, but it feels like it must be someone else eating, not the you you've known for so long? What will you do when no one says, "oh, you're so lucky, you're so skinny" anymore? Who will I be? I hope I can be like you, emcd and Simone, so strong and knowing and sure of yourselves.

Thanks for being here!

emcd   ◻ posted 12-28-1999 12:44 PM

There's a very physical reaction to starvation—I couldn't THINK clearly, did that happen to you? I couldn't concentrate and I felt nervous and insecure all the time. I felt like my head was floating above my body all the time, disconnected and fuzzy. I was cold in August. Sometimes I simply forgot what I had started saying mid-sentence; I could rarely hold a coherent conversation. I was focused on food 24 hours, counting calories in class, at my desk at work, on scraps of paper on the train—I was a mess!

I'm probably a size 5 now, although I still haven't bought new clothes because somehow it makes it too final and REAL if I actually BUY a size 5; but I don't think anyone would notice I've gained weight. I think what they notice is that I look healthier.

One of the things that really made me realize something was wrong with me was that I used to associate "health" with "fat"—one time a friend's mother who I hadn't seen in a while told me that I looked good, my face looked much healthier than last time she had seen me and I immediately started planning a newly restrictive diet for the next day in my head. That was a BAD thing to hear, that I looked healthy—I didn't want health, I wanted gaunt, sick, pale. So I've consciously re-taught my brain to strive for health; now when one of my friends I haven't seen since school says I look great, and I KNOW it's because I've gained weight, I tell my brain, "that's good, love that, say thank you, mean it."

Reenie    posted 12-30-1999 07:16 AM

As a teenager I used to be really skinny. No matter how much I ate, I was just skin and bones. My family used to make terrible comments about my skinnyness, as if it were a disease, and how no man would find me attractive, etc.

When I hit my twenties I put on 20 pounds.

Now I'm 28, am 5 feet 5 inches, and weigh 135 lbs. I live in Norway, and my family lives in Brooklyn; I just visited them. EVERYONE made a comment about how much weight I had gained, as if it were a disease. They were just as critical about my weight now as they were when I was 20 pounds lighter! No matter how fat or thin you are, it doesn't matter what people think, 'cause the only person it should matter to is you. I love my weight now. The only thing I hate about my body is my double chin. Which, by the way, I am considering getting liposuction on! AND that is MY decision. My husband is against it. However, he sees nothing wrong with working out like a maniac, but liposuction...he thinks is for bimbos. I disagree, I think a woman should do whatever she wants with her body.

Moondance    posted 12-31-1999 12:09 AM

emcd, your not wanting to buy new clothes to fit your new (beautiful) body is sort of like my reluctance to write about my eating disorder...it makes it too permanent, gives it a life of its own. Though for you, it's more like recovery you don't want to give a life of its own; for me, it's the anorexia.

Recently, though, I've been writing (and reading) about it like crazy, like I am hungry for knowledge now that I've fed my body; now my mind wants its nourishment too. And my soul wants desperately to express itself, which is probably why I'm here writing to you now. I've filled 12 pages in my diary, and I'm not scared anymore that someone might see it. Let them see it! Let them hear my thoughts and see what I've become and how far I've come! And let them see what my friends are going through this very second. Maybe then they wouldn't tell my friends they look so beautiful when their cheeks are sunken in and they're losing their lives. It makes me so mad, I want to scream.

I guess recovery is gonna take a long time. The good thing is, you know that when your anorexia starts to talk (or scream)

81

you'll be conscious of it, and able to crush it. You're not denying it. I'm not either now, but only six months ago I probably was. And when I couldn't recognize its existence, it had power over me. The thing is, anorexia is not us. It's an evil invader. It's everything that's wrong with our patriarchal society intruding on our minds and hearts.

renee   posted 01-01-2000 05:22 PM

The fact that we have to even discuss this just goes to show you what a major influence society has on our self-image.
It's so sad to hear how many of you have had and have eating disorders. I think it's wonderful though, that the subject is being brought up and that we realize how much talent and energy is wasted on obsessing over weight/appearance. Obviously, today's anorexic model-look is unattainable for most women. The question is, why is it so popular? Why are men attracted to women who look like they haven't hit puberty yet? And why do women buy into it? I find it very hard, myself, to overcome this spoon-fed idea of what I should look like and what beauty is.
It is so sad that so many women (myself included) spend so much time and energy focusing on weight and appearance when there are so many other, equally beautiful parts of our person to concentrate on??

Katie   posted 01-01-2000 07:25 PM

This isn't exactly on the topic that started this discussion, but is there any way of reassuring my friends who think they're too fat? Two in particular worry me (they're both 14). One doesn't complain about her weight, but she skips many meals, then says she feels too nauseated to eat; she's dropped a lot of weight in less than six months. My other friends (and her boyfriend) have tried warning her that this is dangerous, but she says she doesn't feel like eating. The other doesn't diet to my knowlege, but she always talks about how "gross" and "fat", and she's said (only half in jest) that she should follow the example of the one that doesn't eat. We've told her over and over that she isn't fat, but she doesn't believe us. Is there any way to get through to them? I've known them for 5 years, and it worries me to see them do this to themselves.

82

Moondance posted 01-01-2000 08:54 PM

Katie, I would tell your friends that you know how confused they are. Tell them to look around them at all the beautiful different shapes and sizes and colors out there, and ask them why they think only one shape (skinny) is desirable. Maybe that will get them thinking about why they are being sucked into a trap that seeks to paralyze them in fear and misery. Once they start actually thinking about these things, questioning the patriarchy, stop internalizing the skewed, rigid, and constricting values they've been taught, maybe they will start to consciously care for themselves and respect themselves, instead of doing battle with their own bodies.

That's the abstract stuff. You should also tell your parents so that they can give you advice and maybe talk to your friends' parents. Maybe tell a trusted and supportive teacher, counselor, or administrator, or, if you know the parents of the girls who are developing eating disorders, go straight to them. This is a really dangerous and miserable disease, and it's not your responsibility to worry about them.

I'm a few years older than you (17), and I can tell you, all through high school, girls obsess about their bodies and the "fat" that's not there because this society conditions them to do so; I obsessed too, and still do, sometimes. If your friends can stop this eating disorder from taking over their lives now, they will have a much better high school experience, not to mention the fact that they will survive!

bean posted 01-01-2000 10:19 PM

Congrats to all of those who have had the courage to write about their ordeals here. I too have had to deal with an eating disorder in my life, however, quite the opposite from most of the others here. I had to recover (am still recovering) from compulsive overeating.

When I was a child, and through my early teen years, I was very tall and very slender (5 feet 9 and 124 pounds at age 14). But I also had severe scoliosis. I had to have a plaster body cast made for me every 3 months, where these men would literally stretch my body out as much as possible and then slop warm plaster all over my torso. They would always make comments about how perfect my body was (I was only 13 and 14, for God's sake). Later, I ended up having to have a spinal fusion done. and had to wear a 25 pound, unremovable plaster body cast for 9 months.

In addition to the problems created by the scoliosis and the casts and braces, I was raped when I was 15 by a 20-year-old man I had just met. I kept trying to tell him I was only 15 and a virgin, but he kept telling me that no 15-year-old virgin would have a body like that.

Also, my mother grew up very heavy, and was constantly dieting. Every time I put anything in my mouth, she would ask, "Are you sure you really need to eat that?" All of these factors (and probably many more) caused me to attempt to both gain control over and change my body (just as many anorexics and bulimics do). So I began overeating. So here I was gaining weight every day, and hating myself for doing so, and getting depressed, which only caused me to eat more and more. I still haven't lost the weight, but I have gained some control over my eating, and am gaining acceptance for my body.

I have only two more comments to make. First, for those of you who desperatly want to fit into that size 0, think about it; do you really want to be a zero, a nothing? (Believe me, I know that there is a great deal involved, and I am not trying to make a joke or trivialize the situation). Second, as far as expanding the standards of beauty, I truly believe that if society has only one concept of beauty, most of the women will always be lacking. My friend Bethany said it best: "With my luck, if I lived in Rubens' time, I'd look like Kate Moss."

 Simone   posted 01-01-2000 10:19 PM

Reenie: That is the sad thing about society—there are such specific standards that, really, the only way to live up to them is to have plastic surgery done all over your body. Which I'm sure is more common than we want to think about.

I have to admit I've considered liposuction plenty of times. And really, as you mentioned, is it any worse than working out? People justify strenuous workouts by saying they make you healthy; well, there are plenty of people who work out obsessively, which is obviously NOT healthy, and no one thinks twice about this being a problem.

I hope one day every woman can be healthy and happy with her feminine curves. After all, this is how we are engineered to look. A lot of times I get a little self-righteous about "bimbos" who have had liposuctions or boob jobs to look like the advertising patriarchy's heroin-addict-thin "ideal woman." But, goddess, if it comes to starving oneself or going under the knife, I think I'd rather have everyone get plastic surgery. I read that seven out of ten anorexics eventually die from the disease or its results (heart failure, etc.). I doubt that cosmetic surgery would exist if the odds were that bad.

emcd   posted 01-02-2000 02:25 AM

Simone: PLEASE don't get lipo!!! Read above about Kathy Griffin's article in *Glamour* detailing her experience with it; she's an actress and had access to all the best doctors and equipment, and she had to be catheted four times because urine was backing up and running through her bloodstream from complications of the surgery—among various other horrible results—and she didn't even lose one inch! She had the surgery to reach her goal of a size 2 (from her natural, obese size of 4) and it didn't even work. There are plenty of horror stories like hers, but an industry as thriving and profitable as cosmetic surgery does their damnedest to keep its "mistakes" quiet, rest assured. That ANY unecessary surgery should have a mortality rate at all is ludicrous to me.....
Bean: thank you for sharing your story. You sound strong and brave and beautiful. Society tends to extend more sympathy to anorexics than it does to compulsive overeaters when really both disorders stem from the same place...and your point about not striving for "zero" is so true; however it's sad that, as we mentioned before, the world gets increasingly congratulatory and praising as women get thinner, so it's hard not to equate zero with success sometimes.

Moondance   posted 01-02-2000 01:48 PM

I know this isn't exactly what everyone is talking about, but I just have to tell somebody, so I hope it's okay if I tell you guys. After 3 years without it, I FINALLY got my period!! I'm SO happy, I can't tell you. I finally feel normal! Part of me (the old anorexic, intrusive, evil part) is saying, uh oh, that means you're getting fat; but I'm telling that part of me to shut up, because I'm healthy now, I'm a woman, having my period is womanly and healthy!

bean   posted 01-02-2000 01:54 PM

There is a book that I think every woman should read—and it deals with many of the issues discussed in this thread. It is called *Real Beauty* by Kaz Cooke. It is a brilliant, moving and hilarious book about what is "normal"—and looks at everything from body size/shape to menstrual cycles and breast size. The main point is that almost everything is "normal" if it occurs naturally. And she does this while stressing the importance of accepting all types of beauty—fat/thin, short/tall, etc.

emcd   posted 01-02-2000 07:35 PM

I'm so glad the Internet exists right now, because otherwise I don't think I would ever know the extent to which so many of my own experiences are shared by others...

People often feel so alone, like they're the only ones in the world with their particular problems, but really it's just that no one talks about their problems enough. Here, people feel okay about sharing their feelings because it's very anonymous, but we also know that however "imaginary" we all seem to one another, we have to be real too and that means there are real people walking around dealing with the same shit as us.

Anyway, getting my period again was such a hard thing...I didn't get it for 3 years straight either, and I was proud of that at my worst, I reveled in it... sometimes I would get it for like a day really light and I would panic and feel like a failure.... So when I started getting it again for real this year (migraines, four days of blood, cramps, bloating and all) I cried and went through a period (no pun intended) of great depression at first before consciously deciding that I WANTED it, I WANTED to be a mature, normal woman, not a pre-adolescent waif for the rest of my life.

It wasn't until I simply decided for myself that I'd had enough and needed to be happy, not skinny, that I began to get better.

Shan   posted 01-03-2000 06:06 PM

Renee brought something into the conversation that I think bears discussion, and this is the idea of desire as it ties in with body image (I think that she asked why men are attracted to anorexic bodies, specifically). In my own experience, and when I talk to other women who've been affected by eating disorders, they don't have a lot to do with real desire. Most of us, when we're suffering from the worst of an eating disorder, aren't feeling very desirable, and don't much enjoy sex, or any other sexual/sensual contact. The eating disorder takes that away, makes the body feel shameful and dirty. There's a reason for the anorexic's satisfaction in losing her period: menstuation is female, is sexual, is adult, and that's what the eating disorder is often hiding from; I've had at least one friend deal with this.

And I think that men pick up on this: my sense is that men who enjoy anorexic bodies are men who have issues with adult women, who have feelings of inadequacy, sexual or otherwise, of their own, who need to exert power in some way. I have noticed that most men, or at least virtually all men worth being with, tend to consider eating disorders a puzzling and sad thing, and to prefer being with women who enjoy life, and their bodies. And most men actually LIKE breasts and hips and thighs.

I remember a male friend of mine saying of Christy Turlington, "Somebody buy that woman lunch."

This does not mean that larger women get social validation; it doesn't mean that they (we: I've put most of my weight back on) get admiring glances and strangers flirting with them in the checkout line, but, really, is this something that most of us want? But I've been overweight and unhealthy; I've been thin and unhealthy; I'm now pretty much chunky and healthy. At all times I've found that men weren't the issue: I could attract and interest men. More when I was thinner and more vulnerable, yes, but more of them were scary.

Eating disorders can rob us of our goddess-given sexuality, our ownership of our bodies, and of our pleasure. The sensual world is not the prerogative of fashionable bodies.

emcd   posted 01-03-2000 07:28 PM

Very true, Shan—I was completely disinterested in sex when i was anorexic, no desire for it at all, totally in denial that I was even a sexual person or had potential to enjoy sex—it was like a chore for me.

Now that I'm better, it's like a whole new world....

Simone   posted 01-03-2000 08:20 PM

Actually, on the subject of guys liking women rather than stick-figures, I used to think that guys saying they liked curves on their women was a cop-out to trick me into stopping dieting. Irrational, I know, but there were just as many guys (interestingly enough, now that I look back on it, they WERE mostly creepy, controlling, stalker types like Shan mentioned) who thought it was just great that I "cared about being in shape" enough to eat 200 calories a day and exercise for three hours a night.

I still kind of take those "I like women who don't eat rabbit food" comments with a grain of salt, because I know my husband is not going to admit, "Yes, your butt is fat. I really wish you'd hit the treadmill more often." But as my best friend's boyfriend says when she and I obsess about eating, "Marilyn Monroe was a size 14 and nobody would dream of calling her an obese, unattractive whale-woman."

Were we to take as much
pains to be what we ought,
as we do to disguise what we
are, we might appear like ourselves without being at the
trouble of any disguise at all.

• *La Rochefoucauld* •

When a woman becomes a scholar
there is usually something wrong with her sexual organs.

• Nietzsche •

A very little wit is valued in a woman,
as we are pleased with a few words spoken plain by a parrot.

• Jonathan Swift •

A woman,
especially if she has the misfortune of knowing anything,
should conceal it as well as she can.

• Jane Austen •

She was a large woman,
who seemed not so much dressed as upholstered.

• Sir James Barrie •

Have we really come a long way?

How can I know
what I think
unless I see
what I write?

• *Erica Jong* •

A CIRCLE OF WOMEN

Choice and Accommodation

Squeezed in too-narrow theater seats,
I mouth a complaint to my mother.
Don't complain, she says,
it's your own fault.

Sure, like sidewalk ramps,
like who doesn't get into a building:
the legless,
because he chose to go to Da Nang,
because he chose to be point man
on that flawed patrol,

the paralyzed
who dove off the trestle on a dare
despite weekly warnings from his mother,
the drinker who wrapped around a tree
after a party,

handicapped parking
for the emphysemic
toting her oxygen tank after a life
of Lucky Strikes.

Do I say this to my mother?
You all have mothers; does it do any good?

My mother believes in the tines of fate,
that viruses and bacteria are strong invaders,
but she cannot accept that travails of the mind
can seek comfort in the body—that early
stages of fat are insulation against things the mind
can't or doesn't want to face—that fat can keep the world at bay,
can compensate, reorganize what parents
and centuries of society have laid on hard.

Horses are handicapped before they ever
enter the gates, still the gates are made large
enough to accommodate each and all the horses.

But the human world is made for thin.
Cameras prefer it, cars gear their steering wheels
to eliminate a burgeoning gut,
clothes and shoes are made, not to cover and shelter

but to show off Reed Woman. And yet, we are
getting larger even as winds circle the globe—
larger and taller.

Recently I sat in a lecture hall and watched
the audience file in. Looked for the heavy-set,
saw them find a seat and eye it, measuring.
They knew the likelihood of comfort.

I watched them sit at the end of the seat,
gingerly push back and wince.
As the lecture progressed, I checked
and found them all at angles, tilted
to take pain off their hips, or sitting forward
out of the crushing embrace.

I know they are only half-listening
and cannot absorb what they've come to hear.

• *Carolyn, 63* •

I was the oldest of four children and became a mother to others, looking for a mother for myself. I was chubby from age 8, hating the skinny image of my mother who had us all by the age of 27. She tried, but working-full-time parents did not allow much space for attention. I know I sought attention and love through academic achievement, and tried to ignore my body most of my teen and young adult life. I believed in sixth grade that I was not allowed to look in mirrors and primp with the other girls because I was not good enough, and people would laugh.

I lost weight at 14 with my adolescent growth spurt, and resented the physical attention I then got from boys, despite enjoying the attention I craved. I met my husband when I was 19, and a feminist/bisexual radical who weighed 137 but inside was still at the 190 pounds that became my adult weight for many years. I never believed he really loved me, felt I had cheated him by marrying when I was relatively thin then but reverting to the true fat me. We are still married after nearly 24 years, amazingly enough, so maybe I'm wrong.

I decided to take classes in pre-med because it seemed like a logical career choice for someone who had always done well in school. The first year I applied to medical school (after working full time, going to school part time for five years), I was rejected. The adviser told me I wasn't medical school material because I was too fat. I persevered, and after being rejected the next year, decided to give up that dream.

Then the same adviser called and asked me in August if I wanted to go to med school because they had open slots. So I slid in the back door, always feeling second best and that I had to prove myself because I was fat. I survived, and interviewed for residency when I was seven months pregnant. My husband found a seamstress who made some original "fat lady" pregnant suits for me to interview in. This was embarassing but tolerable.

I didn't get accepted into the residencies I applied for, and got a slot in the "scramble" in the desolate spaces of South Dakota. Fortunately, I transferred after a year to Milwaukee (Wisconsin being the state with the heaviest average female weight), and I was practically svelte compared to many. I did well there, even got chief resident of the year, but still suffered with feeling "not good enough," grounded in the reminder in the mirror that I didn't fit the image of a doctor (athletic, healthy, thin and smart, beautiful wouldn't hurt, either).

I took a job in an area where my family lived, and settled down for eight years, doing my job, winning friends and patients. Inside, I still quaked at the thought that someone would figure out I really wasn't "good enough," and would burst my bubble. I became board certified (grueling oral exams) at five weeks post partum after my third child, glad to fit into a suit of sorts that wasn't tailormade. As an obstetrician/gynecologist, I met many women who were able to reveal their inner fears to me, another fat woman, and felt as though I had found my niche. (I had plenty of thin patients, too!)

Then the nightmare of not being good enough came up again, after a difficult birth/injury case. The hospital started a peer review process, which my medical group continued, and this week I quit my job in a negotiated settlement. The pain of rejection and failure is still very fresh, and I am having a hard time not getting stuck in a hole of self-hate that started with my negative body image. The irony is that I just lost 50 pounds over the last six months, and was starting the path to better health when all hell broke loose.

I expect I'll still be able to work somewhere, but the pain will never be totally gone. I'm hoping to maintain the weight loss while looking for a healthier, more supportive work setting (what's wrong with working 80–90 hours a week and not having time for yourself?) and I will find a way to help other women continue to try to love themselves as I work on the same goal.

• *Lynne, 45* •

I had anorexia nervosa last year, and so did two of my friends. My head rang true with one fact: I was fat, disgusting, morbidly obese at 5 feet 9 inches and 130 pounds. It hurt me to hear others say that I was skinny, because I knew that was a lie. Even while I watched my best friend sink deeper and deeper into the darkness and was scared to death of losing her, I couldn't see my problem.

Luckily, my mommy caught my anorexia before I had lost any weight (which means that I was never clinically anorexic). As we started discussing what a normal, healthy body looks like, I realized how far off the images that the media portrays are. I used to believe that models like Kate Moss and actresses like Jennifer Aniston and Calista Flockhart were the norm, but now I know better.

Now that I realize the affect the media has had on me, I have vowed to commit my life to preventing this from happening to another generation. For we have the power and the right to take back our confidence!

• *Molly, 15* •

A Look Back at A Pattern of Food and Dieting

The box, in a rather dilapidated state, had a permanent place in a corner of the basement laundry room. Having survived moves from graduate school apartment to duplex to starter house to this home of 30 years beside a lake, it was easy to ignore until a remodeling job forced me to take a look. Through the years I had tossed recipes into this carton thinking that some day I would organize them all—yellowed clippings from the smalltown Indiana newspaper where my Mom worked as copyeditor, shiny photos of gourmet dishes from upscale magazines, and recipes clipped from the food section of major city newspapers. With a wintry afternoon ahead of me and a cup of tea, I finally started the job of sorting and, in the process, learned a lot about myself and my attitudes toward food.

I was always interested in food, and as a child of the Depression belonged to the "clean plate" club. Homemade desserts were the reward, and I made sure that I was in line for the fresh peach cobbler or heavenly chocolate cake. As I sorted my recipe stash, a pattern became apparent, with various foods representing the decades—tuna casserole and sugary Jell-o salads from the 1950s to polenta and grilled chicken of the 1990s. Another pattern emerged from this hodgepodge collection—I seemed to have had a diet for every decade as well. Grapefruit diets, liquid diets, exchange diets—I tried them all. Memories of emotionally draining diet meetings—in a strip mall office in a city, a YWCA classroom in the suburbs, and various physicians' offices—came tumbling back. Some of the diet plans were very strange and almost all made certain foods taboo. I was constantly seeking the secret formula to losing weight, but never found it. The dieting regimens of my life were not only a waste of time and money but also resulted in unhealthy eating habits.

Today, I don't diet. I have come to terms with my weight and work to keep it under control with exercise and healthy eating. There are no forbidden foods. I have learned that I feel much better when I eat lighter meals and drink plenty of water. I am still an ardent "foodie" and read cookbooks the way others read novels. I indulge my interest in cuisine by reviewing restaurants and preparing special dishes for others. I look for the freshest foods and find a trip to the farmers' market a treat; the mounds of alternating vegetables and fruits present a lush, colorful palette. As a food critic, I have learned not to clean up my plate but to "taste and waste." A taste is often enough, and I no longer try to mimic current media personalities as I did when I was younger. I have found success in other areas and my exact size is no longer a daily concern. I applaud the use of models of all sizes as well as various age groups in advertising. When I look to the women I admire, I realize I am interested in what they have to say, their sense of humor, their philosophy of life—not their size.

• *Doris, 64* •

My body used to be something I climbed trees, rode bikes, and built forts with. My body became, in my mind, my biggest enemy. I felt awkward and ungainly before puberty. After puberty, all I saw was fat, but I look back at pictures of that unhappy girl and I don't see any of the outrageous obesity that I thought was there. I see a sad-eyed girl who thought she was ugly, and *that's* why they didn't love me. I struggled with my weight, food, and self-image ever since I realized how highly "beauty" was prized. I felt like third prize. My early breasts embarrassed me. My round tummy shamed me. My voracious appetite humiliated me.

"You have such a pretty face..." I was always told, and there was a large unspoken BUT. But you need to lose weight. I tried Medifast, Weight Watchers, Richard Simmons, Cocaine, starving, Jenny Craig, threats, and promises. I always fantasized that if I were thin, then "they" would all be sorry...all the men that said, "You are a really cool person, but..." "You'd be so hot if... ." I'd make them weep.

I joined Overeaters Anonymous in 1995 and promptly lost 90 pounds. I still hated myself. My weight loss forced me to admit that there was a lot more going on than excess weight. I regained 70 pounds, and I am now trying to love myself the way I am right now, today. I still want to lose weight, but more for health reasons. I am a beautiful, talented, creative, loving woman, no matter how big my ass is.

• *Laura, 34* •

I have a love/hate relationship with Weight Watchers: it helped me lose weight but now that I am no longer an active participant, I cannot seem to "shake" the obsessing about food, what I eat, etc. I am trying to let it go, but it is difficult.

I have very recently discovered that what I weigh and how I look is not the key to inner happiness. I think it is a big fat lie! I lost 28 pounds, was thinner than I have been since I graduated from college 14 years ago, and I felt even worse than I did before I lost the weight. I felt obsessed with my appearance and my weight, and totally neglectful of my inner self. It felt like a very hollow victory. I do not advocate being overweight, but it makes me wonder and question how great it really was to lose the weight. On the plus side, I conquered something that had bothered me for a while, and made me feel like I could control my eating.

My doctor was happy, but it did nothing to change my low self-concept. I am busy working on self-love currently, instead of my appearance and weight. I would not change anything about my body. My task is to love the body that I have. My experience with weight loss taught me that it wouldn't change my feelings about myself. Also, I am becoming aware that my body is constantly changing and I do not want to go crazy trying to fight with nature.

• *Jana, 35* •

The Starving Woman in Four Parts

Part 1
At twenty-four I ate
one potato a day for three weeks,
a microwaved wrinkled turd
shriveling, empty, flat like me
and my husband so proud of my rejecting
and deflating

At twenty I ate nothing in October.
After class I'd drift to dizzy sleep
my hipbones little unshucked shrimps poking the mattress springs
my eyes growing fast as cancer,
big in a tight, wan face
I hadn't taken a shit in weeks
my dormmates commended my success

At fifteen Nancy and I did the banana diet
(three one-banana meals daily)
the sunflower seed diet (unlimited woody, gum-jabbing seeds)
the chicken diet (three one-wing meals daily)
the laxative diet, crapping out every last morsel
Our collarbones lifted the spaghetti straps of our prom dresses
Our breasts rolled like small firm olives between our boyfriends' fingers

Part 2
During the starving I get dizzy, organized
Listlessly I make lists:
five favorite foods to consume when the starving is over
ten nails to polish
fifteen miles to run
twenty hair curlers to buy
thirty jokes to laugh at
forty days and nights to rain on a man

Part 3
Suddenly I cannot get enough food, or talking, or debts, or daiquiris, or freedom, or earrings, or talk shows, or long mornings on the toilet reading Cosmo.
The pacing sets in, pacing of the bedroom, dormroom, apartment cell, a con-
tainer of whatever, hot or cold in my hands, the strongest zoo lion contained in
the smallest cage, pacing to her racing heart, eyes concealing nothing.

Part 4
The cell-filling begins, crowding in, invading
my still-starving, bursting womanhood:
my hips become ripe plums mashing into the mattress
my breasts brim over my bra
my collarbones sink like an island
my stomach pulls its horsehead forward
my benign eyes melt waxlike into a fleshy face.

To face facing the face is the last part
known now by heart.

• *Kate, 37* •

It was the year Karen Carpenter died, and about the same time that Cherry Boone O'Neill published her important little book, *Starving for Attention*. 1983. The disease now so commonly acknowledged was only a whisper. Then came those haunting photos of a gaunt and wasted beauty on the front pages of about every magazine on the rack. The articles spoke of how Karen's resonant alto voice was great until the very end of her all-too-short 33 years of life.

I remember that year very well, especially now at Christmas time when Karen's voice is piped through the music in the malls and the department stores—that wonderful Christmas album—and then the tears come to my eyes.

It was that year that our bright and talented and extraordinarily beautiful daughter decided, out of the blue, to stop eating. It started with fussing at breakfast and went to throwing away the lunch bag I so carefully prepared with all the good stuff, fresh vegetables, fruit, whole grain bread. Then it went to being absent from dinner to believing that drinking water and even the smell of food had calories. In three months this 5 feet 4 inch, 125 pound joyful spirit went to a sad little waif, 85 pounds of flesh hanging off bone.

The thinner she got, the more adulation she got from peers, boys especially. Grown men seemed to love it even more. She was near death when we finally got her in the hospital that would stabilize her. She was out of the hospital in a couple of months, but it would be five years before she would be "out of the woods," and five more before she would be comfortably sailing the turbulent waters of this addiction.

She was born the year we landed a man on the moon, but in 1983 about as much was known about anorexia as about the man IN the moon. She was 14. Those afflicted were given a 30 percent chance of survival, maybe. The news was terrifying! It was mostly for young women, and if they did survive, they would most likely not be able to bear children. Eating disorders had been discovered. Out of the closet, so to speak.

Closet eaters. I recall that Karen's body was found in a closet. Jackie Barille wrote of her addiction, *Confessions of a Closet Eater*.

As our darling was disappearing before our very eyes, we searched every avenue for answers. Money was not a problem. We sought and found the best care that money could buy. We were referred to the "top guy" in a major southern California university. He referred our daughter to his psychiatric facility, where she only got worse, until there was nothing to do but put her in a "real" hospital with hyper-alimentation to stabilize her physically. That worked, but it was only the beginning of a very, very long and anguishing recovery. It was a whole-family event, only we didn't know it at the time. It was a larger community event in reality. We found out somewhere in the process that the doctor we had selected was one of Karen's doctors. We were part of *his* learning process too.

All during the early days, the maddening questions came. Why? Why is she doing this to herself? Anger: why is she doing this to us? She was at once willful and nasty, and at the same time childlike and helpless. I searched every possible resource. I delved into evidence that most anorexics had been sexually abused, or molested, or incested. I rummaged into the past and remembered at one time I had a teenage boy for a babysitter when she was little. I asked her if anyone had touched her where they should not have touched her. She did not recall anything like that. And there were the other "suspects," her devoted father and two younger brothers. Her admiring and sexually demanding older boyfriend of the moment. No, not that! Who was the culprit? Whose was the "fault?"

I considered that if it was our fault, then it would have to be our cure; but the reality was, she was in charge. And no one seemed to have the answer. The problem was that our picture was not her picture. When she looked in the mirror at skin and bones she saw FAT! Imagine that.

Confusion reigned. "Helpful" friends and relatives do not realize how near death they came when they would suggest to me that she would "get over it." Another would say, "Just wait, when she gets to be 24, something magic will happen." SHE WILL BE DEAD BY THEN, DAMMIT!

One young man comes to mind in particular. My husband and I were on our way to take Monica to meet Jackie Barille to pick her brains and heart and soul. It was about two days before we were to get her into the hospital. We were having lunch at a restaurant in a popular mall. Monica sat and watched us eat. When she left the table briefly to go to the ladies' room, the waiter came over to let us know just how absolutely beautiful our daughter was. Seeing the rage in my eyes and fully realizing that this young man was about to have a near death experience...her father plopped money on the table, grabbed my arm, and ushered me out the door.

This story has a happy ending. It did come to pass that we all got through it. Recently, I passed by a wall of windows exposing every possible piece of exercise equipment with muscular, fit young men and nubile young women aboard, burning away. One woman in particular took my eye. Oh, she was magnificent! The very image of the tight body, wailing away on an exercycle, facing a full-length mirror. She was watching a TV monitor with headphones on, listening to a Walkman strapped to her waist, munching on an apple. I didn't know whether to laugh or cry.

• *Mary, 60* •

I am a healthy, happy, normal 24-year-old woman, just beginning my second year of graduate studies in music. I am a cellist, and enjoy performing in several concerts each month around northern California. I teach music classes to hundreds of students and love every minute of it. I work out three times a week at my gym, and when I feel like relaxing, I draw or write poems in my journal. I have a wonderful boyfriend who loves me for who I am, and many people could only dream about making a living by playing music. However, my life was not always so idyllic.

I was born in Kansas City, Missouri to two parents who weren't ready for a daughter, I guess. From the age of 2, I was raised by my grandparents, two ex-New Yorkers who gave me the world on a silver platter. I was their princess for 18 years. I adored them and was adored, unconditionally. I graduated high school with honors. I excelled in extra-curricular activities; I played on the varsity tennis team. Then I moved to Chicago to go to college. I wanted to be a writer. Somewhere in between 1993 (high school graduation) and 1997 (college graduation) the sweet, confident, corn-fed Midwestern girl became a hardened, icy, urban shell. I'd gone through two major programs of study in a whirlwind of papers, parties, concerts, part-time jobs and el rides—all in the course of four short years. And somewhere in between I lost myself. I was an "anorexic" (or so I was told).

Everyone wondered, "how could this happen?" Alison was so smart, so bright, so cheerful. Why would she do this to herself? How could she be so vain as to diet herself to this corpse-like shell? My friends and family asked me, but of course I had no answers for them. No answers because I thought they were nuts—in my mind, I looked no different at 85 pounds than I did at 145—they just wanted to disrupt my routine, make me fat.

Looking back, I'm sure my grandfather's death played a huge role in my developing anorexia. Actually, he died very suddenly, and I was the only one there when he had a stroke and lapsed into a coma—the last words he ever spoke were to me, and they were strange, drug-induced mumblings that scared me so. For weeks after he died, I never slept, I just lay in bed replaying the scattered images of his lifeless face, nose bleeding from the tubes inside, his body thin and wasted.

Night after night, I prayed so hard that I actually felt I had my own private line to heaven. Days I spent running endless circles around the local junior high school track, because you can't cry if you're running, I figured out. I methodically drank two quarts of water afterward, then waited until 7 p.m. when I would eat one steamed zucchini and half a grapefruit, then I would go to bed and start praying again. It was a hazy summer. Then school started again, and my own slow death began to consume me. And my boyfriend broke up with me because my depression over my grandfather's death was too much for him. To make a very long story short, Alison left her body, and a mean, nasty voice in her head took over for a year. A voice that wouldn't let her eat more than 500 calories per day. A voice that told her that after she ate or drank anything (except water) she must run one mile for each 100 calories. A voice that told her she looked better in a size 0 than a size 4, but still not pretty. Strange, considering that if Alison had been consulted on the matter of body size, she would've probably remembered feeling absolutely gorgeous in her size 10 homecoming dress, on the night of her first kiss.

Now, almost three years later, I have been through therapy groups, psychologists, and clothing sized 0 to 14 and back to 10, and I wouldn't trade anything for my experiences. I went from a weak, scared, mean little girl who couldn't even hold her cello up, to a strong, confident, smiling woman preparing to give a solo recital on October 29. I have my life back, and I'm making good decisions for myself now because I already know the outcomes of letting negativity take over, and I promised myself (and my grandmother) that I would never go down those roads again. I love myself (and my body) now; every lump, every fleshy curve, every pimple is gorgeous, because it is mine, and I am gorgeous. I am alive.

• *Alison, 24* •

Beauty 101

"You can't be too thin," said my father to me as a child. He'd hug me to him and add, "You can't be too rich, either, but never mind. I'll take care of the riches." He'd sit me on his knees, and we'd play magic kingdom, with him the pasha and I his favorite slave girl. I adored him. I wanted to be a princess. My mother, reed-svelte at 5 feet 2 inches and 100 pounds, was his queen.

This occurred in the fifties—when women were a successful man's accoutrements, like a British briefcase. Daddy, who relished commenting about passing women, female guests at parties, devalued a "dish," to a "bimbo" if she bore five extra pounds. "Women are like stocks in a fluctuating market," he'd say.

A skinny, bony, pre-pubescent stick, I devoured my mother's fashion magazines. At 13, I shot up to 5 feet 5, and expanded, in three months, from 100 to 130 pounds. Daddy expressed critical dismay; Mummy cried. Diet, they pronounced. Body weight was a matter of will, of control. I yearned for the physical starkness my parents prescribed, but I felt famished all the time.

A friend, infectious intestinal flu, saved the day. Vomiting, I discovered, reduced me two pounds overnight. Half an inch validated by the handy tape measure I carried secretly, a daily index of my fluctuating net worth. Experimentally, I stuck my finger down my throat after my next over-abundant meal. Disgusting, I thought, as the undigested dinner flooded the toilet bowl, but then so was I. At last, in an out-of-control world, something I could control. Vomiting made my throat sore; a remedy to be employed sparingly. For a while, it worked. Purging brought me closer to the perfection and purity my parents advocated. I lost four, six, eight, twelve pounds. That sufficed, I decided, and returned to regular eating. I didn't realize my control was becoming an addiction beyond my control, that the freedom I sought desperately would increasingly elude me.

Ashamed and guilty, I told no one. If emotional illness is the sum total of our secreted selves, by age 15, I was gravely ill. An academic overachiever who anointed toilet bowls, I couldn't go to friends' homes for delicious overnight stays—someone might discover my secret, might report me to my parents. I couldn't attend slumber parties, or go on camping trips with friends.

Slowly, I came to see that my bulimia, a word not common currency then, had trapped me. That it, not I, nor even my judgmental parents, owned me. For two years I stopped inducing vomiting. My weight, now entirely dependent on diet, fluctuated wildly. Size 4 suits morphed into size 6, size 8, size 6, and 4 again. I was my dressmaker's delight.

Years later, my father told me he and my mother had known, but decided not to say anything. "You know how I respect privacy," he said smugly. In my thirties then, I replied that if he'd respected my privacy, ever, self-control would not have become an obsession. If he'd acknowledged my teenager's natural proclivity to chunkiness, I might have followed his lead. Probably would have held my self too sacred to desecrate. "That's one way of looking at it," he pronounced, uncomfortable, as ever, with contradiction.

At 18, I was raped by a relative. My account of the event was disbelieved. In a flash, I went back to bulimia. Out of the fire back to the frying pan. If women, as society seemed to suggest, were intended for abuse, surely I could do it myself. Now it wasn't just dinner, but all meals. Compulsively, I ate box after box of pretzels, cookies, or chips bought out of summer job earnings. Pint after pint of ice cream, sherbet, fruited instant sundaes.

Now I can consider the harm I did myself, own my past events. My present hypoglycemia probably arises from those years of sugar and insulin abuse. Now I can reflect on the price I paid, acknowledge what I missed. Bulimia was a demanding master, requiring one to sacrifice life itself to its voracious, always open mouth. Enough was never enough. It amazes me I never became anorexic. I couldn't appreciate fully my beautifully shaped body until psychotherapy and friends in the Women's Movement and love set me free. I never yearned to be a stick again. Women were intended to be lumpy.

Nor do I blame myself. Others, my parents, my society, set up the pathological syndrome I became slave to. It's hard at 13 to disregard social forces surrounding you. It's easier to submit—after all, I'd already been a slave for Daddy. Why not for male society's insistence on slimness? I no longer feel guilt or shame, but pride that in the midst of family confusion and adolescent chaos, I somehow found an exit. And a path I travel often into myself where, amongst the signs of aging 54 years brings, I find myself beautiful.

• Shelby, 54 •

At 14 I learned the power
I had
as an autonomous
skinny thing,
shoving speed
up my nose in the mornings
as my mother sipped her coffee
downstairs
I'd turn the music up
louder
so she couldn't hear
my deep snort
like her
muffled phone talk
I heard
through the walls
that separated us
daily

she never knew why
I was losing the weight
never asked who
I was losing it
for

because seven years
had to pass
for me to hear
we all lose
parts of ourselves

to take up
less space
in the world
so our thighs don't impose,
our bellies won't invade space,
our selves can't incline to
claim territory—

I crouched small
on that linoleum floor
where I clenched

my fists while I drew
small red threads
on my inner wrists
over and over
until the
straight-stitch design
looked good enough
to do the job
the aspirin
couldn't finish

girls at
14 aren't quick enough,
aren't fast enough
to live
this life of cries
for help
so I let the bathwater
take me
and the blood
down the drain

to a place I never knew
I'd be,
that adolescent ward
which became my home,
a vacation of sorts,
with the bandages covered
by leather straps,
an IV making more marks
on the flesh-on-bone arm
of one tough cookie
who thought this was
right out of the movies

until the doors shut
behind the gurney
and a dead bolt
made it quite clear
I was no longer
my own
wanting-to-be-woman

but a scared
tiny animal
hiding under
sheets
waiting for the cough
from the next bed
so I could remind
myself
I was not alone

there were other kids
in that hall
of white-on-white—
a 12-year-old boy
from Napa State
who called everyone
Son
in the same voice
they used on him.

A 13-year-old girl
who used sex
as her weapon
of choice
until she threw fists
at the nurses as
they yelled for us
to go
back to our rooms

we shared
one-on-one
so we could
tell our bedtime stories,
make our heirarchy of pain,
compare scars,
tally up
suicide attempts
make notches
for every abuse
we inflicted

on our bodies
we bore
knowledge
of years far
greater
than ours,
wisdom
nobody
could understand
but each other

new friends became
the only thing
we looked forward to
in the
get up-shower-dress-exercise-take meds-
draw-group sessions-family sessions-
you'll-go-up-a-level-if-you-don't-give-us-crap-days

in which we drew
drug paraphernalia,
rock band logos,
and laughed as we
marked up
mug shots of those RNs
we loved to hate

like ourselves.

• *Valerie, 24* •

I remember being about 8 years old, and being pushed to lose weight, cut down on the sweets, and being compared to my skinnier, younger sister. Things became even more difficult as a teenager. Diet after diet, a bout of anorexia, and still I was "fat" (the term my family used). When I graduated high school, I remember feeling unbearably ugly and fat. The sad thing was, I was wearing a pair of jeans sized 32.

This is not fat. This is average from what I have been able to see. My self-esteem never really improved, the ugly voices were still in my head telling me to lose weight, "suck in that gut," don't eat that chocolate. I ended up being pregnant at age 19, and gained a lot of weight, to just over 240 lbs. Before the pregnancy I was 168 pounds.

That was four years ago. With each passing year I have continued to put on weight, and now weigh more than when I was pregnant. This is a guess, as I have stopped weighing myself.

The strangest thing happened along the way: I began to love myself. I began to develop a realistic self-image. I know I am fat. This is one of many parts I have learned to accept about myself. I love myself, for the first time in my life, warts and all. It is ironic that it took me becoming obese to really see myself for who I am. Also, being fat has helped me to become the person I am today. And I do like this person.

• *Christina, 23* •

My mother always wanted me to be beautiful. She told me that cleanliness and beauty were closely related. She wanted me to be thin. I wasn't thin. I was a chubby little girl who liked to eat. She tried to monitor everything that went into my mouth. She didn't have a lot of success with that, because I became quite adept at getting extra food behind her back at every opportunity. Although she wasn't able to fully monitor my input, she did achieve a measure of success in monitoring my output.

My mother believed in frequent enemas, confiding in me how important it was to be clean and beautiful. "Clean and beautiful women are happy," she repeatedly told me. She let me know that she was there to teach me how to be happy. The enemas were always given in my parents' tiny bathroom with the green tile and peeling grout. The enema bag was red with a black rubber hose attached. The part that she inserted into my body was white and about 5 inches long.

I remember standing next to her in that cramped space watching her fill up the bag with hot water and soapsuds. She would use a plain bar of Ivory soap and fiercely rub it over and over in the palms of her hands until the water was soapy and frothy. She had this very determined look on her face. She looked like she was deeply involved in a very important job and she was going to do it efficiently. I was always frightened. I knew the routine. But we were a mother-daughter team in this mission. I knew that I was really going to get cleaned out, and I really wanted to be clean and beautiful and happy.

I nervously would watch the clear hot water turn white and frothy. I was always unhappy. I felt dirty and ugly. I always had the hope that after my mother accomplished the goal of a "good enema," that maybe I would feel happier. I knew that the white soapy water would wash out everything inside of me that wasn't supposed to be there. I submitted to this ritual over and over with full cooperation.

When the red bag was finally filled and bulging with the hot soapy water, she'd prime the hose until she could see a few drops of the fluid coming out of the nozzle. She hung up the red bag high on the showerhead with a wire hanger. She put the toilet seat down and then sat down on it. I would then take my clothes off and lie face down across her lap. She would then insert the tube into me and unclamp the little silver piece that held the flow back. I could feel the hot soapy water running swiftly into my body. I was always very quiet until my stomach began to hurt as the water quickly filled me up.

The begging started when my stomach pain became unbearable. I would start screaming wildly and beg her to stop. She would never stop until all the hot clean water was inside of me. Mom would yell, "Hold it in!! Hold it in!!!" I would yell back, "I can't hold it in!! Please, please let me go!!" I would always become hysterical, but she held her grip on me firmly. No amount of screaming and begging stopped the rush of water threatening to explode my body and mind. My mother stopped only when the red bag was empty.

I've struggled with an eating disorder for most of my life. I binged and purged for 20 years, almost to the point of death. I wanted to be clean and beautiful, and I just couldn't hold it in.

• *Mahala, 50* •

I had determined that I was fat at age 11, though pictures reveal my stringbean build. Nevertheless, for 23 years, dieting gave me something to concentrate on when life got tough. If it got really tough, extreme dieting was in order.

Move away to college?
Starve away four sizes until adjustment comes.

Break up with a boyfriend?
Starve until my friends comment wryly about playing the piano on my spine.

Divorce?
Starve until my tailbone sticks out farther than my butt.

The voice helped. It coached constantly, even in my sleep. It was my cheer-leader when I stuck with the program, my taskmaster when I didn't. Periodi-cally, I wondered if those magazine articles about anorexia had anything to do with me.

Do you know what anorexia gets you?

Power. POWER.
Power to say to the world,
fuck you, world,
I don't need to eat. That basic body function is beneath me.
I have the self-control to overcome nature.
Power to look in the mirror, get on the scale, and notice a difference.
This is tangible.
I can watch myself disappear. Can an alcoholic or a compulsive gambler say that about their addiction?
And the disappearance is gradual, subtle. No one notices. If they do, they don't say a word.
They're afraid.

But I got more than just power.
I got bone-chilling cold, curable only with lots of clothes and blankets or, on hot summer days, by sitting in the sunny car with the windows mostly closed.
I got a headache that raged for years.
I got blurred vision.
I got bones sticking out at angles, casting obscene shadows on my body.
I got bruises everywhere, including my ass from sitting down, my joints from lying down.
I got insomnia.
I got a chronic cramping bellyache.

I got diarrhea and constipation.
I got tingling, numb hands, feet, and face from lack of circulation.
I got too weak to stand up out of a chair.
I got a radiating pain in my solar plexus, as my body tried to digest my organs for want of nourishment.
I got admiration from women I encountered.

Imagine. You get to have all this and no one gives you shit; in fact, they're jealous!

I went to lunch with a friend once—I wore lots of clothing, just my long stick hands poking out from my sweatshirt sleeves. Underneath my shirt, a corrugation of ribs, a down-covered back, gooseflesh arms.

I ordered: "Dinner salad, but don't put anything on the plate but lettuce. No tomato, no cucumber, no dressing—just plain lettuce with two lemon wedges, please."

The waitress, bless the little idiot, complimented me with, "I wish I had your willpower."

Are you blind?! I nearly shrieked.

Normal people do not look like this!

Normal people do not go into restaurants and pay money for naked lettuce!

Maybe she envied a life like mine. I wonder if she would have enjoyed contorting herself in bed, such that the skin of one body part never touched the skin of another. No finger may touch its neighbor. The skin above the hinge of the armpit must not make contact with the skin below.
Ankles, knees, thighs, to remain unnaturally separated.
Body parts touching reminded me of how fat I was.

If she knew, would she also have envied the sheer terror of the daily shower? Of sitting alone under the prickling stream with her own repulsive naked body image? Having to touch it to wash.

My friends didn't admire; they feared. They would tender, "If you need to talk, I'm here." But the possibility that a confrontation might cause me to seek a more efficient way to disappear frightened them. They held their tongues and watched.

Help me! I inwardly screamed.

But I didn't want them to help me stop starving,
I wanted them to help me reconstruct my fucked-up life.

My 5-and-a-half-year-old daughter ruined all my fun.
"Mom, I know I can't do anything about it, but sometimes when you don't take care of yourself, I'm afraid you're going to die, and you can't die, because me and Danny are just kids, and we need you. I mean, we have dad, but that's not the same, he's not...We need a mom."

In the end, my heart defeated me. I had always thought that if anything caved in, it would be my will. I had never considered that my body might eventually quit, and I had proudly pushed it to its very limits. Now my heart betrayed me, beating in thready arhythmia. I was clinically informed that I had two choices:

I could stop,
or I could die. Period.
But I have kids.
I had one choice.

Look the demon in the eye and he will disappear. I can't help you if you won't help me. A starving mom is as bad as a drunk mom. Let it go. Let it go. Let it go. I look down and I see a skinny me, and it's the real me, and if I eat, if I gain weight, I'm killing her.

She's not the real you. She's the you who couldn't cope with the world. She's dead. You don't need to be her any more.

I don't need to be her any more.

I do not need to be her any more.

• *Kathleen, 40* •

119

My belly button is gone. It's been eradicated by the being that grows inside me. The being whose pending arrival has me bouncing across a psychotic prenatal spectrum, at one end of which is expectant mother elation, and at the other is the question, "When can I start dieting again?"

Garden variety feelings of angst, excitement, and tenderness fall near to the sane end, metamorphosing into resentment and outright terror as the line separating the two distinct states of being moves away from health and toward dysfunction.

As a pregnant bulimic pondering a due date that's four days away, I look back on the last nine months with a peculiar, curious awe. Something larger than me—with a self-image that's not inextricably tied to a number on the scale—has carried me through what could have easily been 40 weeks of intense self-hatred.

No obstetrician can explain or remedy the nausea that comes not from morning sickness but from learning that the eight pounds you gained in three weeks is here to stay and is absolutely beyond your control. Or the anxiety-pitted depressions that come not from hormonal swings but from the realization that no you can't go on a french-fry-greasy-burger-peanut-butter-parfait spree because it's impossible to purge now. The baby's too big, and pushing on one's stomach to evict the injurious calories probably isn't too helpful for a fetus that lies just inches below.

I wonder if other pregnant women are like this—fraught with obsessions that I thought I had under control, until one day last summer I peed on a stick, and it came back with a second pink line through it.

Being pregnant and having an eating disorder are diametrically opposed conditions, and my brain has split down the middle to accommodate both states. A totally different set of emotions and tribal rules have jurisdiction over each, and there is no cross-over whatsoever. I've spent the last three seasons trying to find a magic point where they intersect, and I keep coming up dry. Empty. Still ravenous with cravings just to feel normal for five minutes.

Normal would be not counting every calorie—every single solitary unit measured in heat that passes through my lips. Normal would be discovering that chicken wings are not inscribed with the numbers 666, sure to send me down into a flaming fat hell. Normal would be actually wanting to feed my baby all she needs regardless of what happens to my body because of it.

So why did I even submit myself to the weight-gaining rigors of pregnancy?

Because I thought I could handle it. I was sure I could overcome that fear of taking up too much space in the world and trade it in for sweet maternal bliss. Because I thought it would be possible to stop searching for an identity externally and maybe even find one in my unborn child.

Ironically, it is in facing these issues that I have come to see myself in my protruding belly. Because before pregnancy, any painful exploration was easily pre-empted by food, wine, cigarettes and marijuana. Not anymore. Pregnancy has forced me to look at my true reflection, no frills included—bareness in all of its human glory.

• *Lizabeth, 34* •

I'll Tell You Why

She has become stoic,
so disconnected from her feelings
that she renders herself after a
Spartan.
Her stomach under her skin
is like a fox under his shirt
gnawing, growling low.
The wound, ignored, seeps blood.

Her frame attenuates,
ectomorphic,
nervous as a stem during
the height of a storm.
How she strives for tragic, sullen,
surface beauty, and beyond that,
for sickness, a breakdown,
a final excuse,
and the inability to explain.

Fasting, she atones for her guilt,
she falls too shy of perfection,
an angel with torn wings
thrust
toward a tumultuous descent.

Does she want to be so thin
she disappears?
Eventually, the knobs and stripes of
bone show, a dark down develops.
She's almost flimsy enough to be
transparent now.

At this stage she has again
dislodged emotion.
She is passive as Zen.

She no longer taunts anger
until it slaps her silly.
Futility can go lord itself
over somebody else.
Her tenderness has
dissolved like sugar in water.

Yes, she has surpassed all the
trouble she's caused herself
and she is not in the least
hungry

• Lisa, 28 •

Goddess by Mattel

This is the Beginning:

Can we really believe that it is all Barbie's fault? It seems to me to be simplifying things to blame an epidemic of eating disorders on a doll, however oddly proportioned she might be. We have an epidemic of morbidly obese Americans as well. Presumably those people who balloon out are exposed to the same drumbeats and images of the ideal female figure as those who choose to eat too little. So? Barbie arrived on the scene at about the same time as the Women's Movement. The point about Barbie for little girls is that Barbie CAN DO ANYTHING. BE ANYTHING. BE ANYBODY. She can be an astronaut. She can run a horse ranch. She can fly. She can have dozens of friends of differing ethnicities to pal around with. She can be the Secretary of State. Heck, she can be President.

Barbie and her friends have briefcases and stethoscopes to play with. Barbie knows that the world is full of choices for adult women, at least in the USA. Before Barbie, and admittedly I am long before Barbie, most little girls were given baby dolls with heavy implications that this was to be their destiny.

Barbie is not the only image of womanhood we are exposed to growing up. Those of us who revere the Virgin Mary see her swathed in blue cloth from head to bare toe—needing only one more layer to delight the Taliban. Vanity of Vanities, the female body is shameful and should be covered up and denied. Don't let your daughter delight in her loveliness as she matures, lest she become vain and (God forbid) promiscuous. It's scary raising girls, you know—the world is a dangerous place for them.

This is the Middle:

Food has always been a means of control. Vague outside forces make the rules, some written down centuries ago. One mustn't eat swine. Never eat shrimp. Eat a hamburger on Friday and roast in hell forever. (There seems to have been a dispensation for that one.) Fast on this day and that day. Give up candy for Lent and score multiple points. The Church used to canonize holy ladies who mortified the flesh, often to the point of starvation and terminal illness. The philosopher, Simone Weil, is approaching beatified status among some circles, and she starved herself to death in the forties, ostensibly for spiritual reasons. Nowadays it isn't always religion, it's our secular pontiffs who send out charts showing how much we SHOULD weigh, whatever our bone structure or genetic makeup. Don't ever eat eggs, they whine, lest you keel over from a heart attack. No, that's not right, we just discovered that eggs are okay. It's carbohydrates, or no organics, or whatever, that are bad for us and we are bad people if we don't follow the ever-changing rules. This barrage of images and directives and stories about food are what we are exposed to constantly from the day we refuse to eat our peas and are sent to bed without our supper.

Food is love. Food is control. I have a set point seemingly set in granite, yet I cannot stand Weight Watchers. I cannot stand anybody telling me what to put into my mouth. Or not to. Oh, I know from personal experience that eating or not eating is a way of maintaining control over my own body. My own autonomy. I also know from personal experience that fasting makes funny things happen as glycogen takes over in the brain. First there is a sense of euphoria and exhilaration, a burst of energy. Then it gets better and better until it approaches the Rapture of the Deep that divers encounter. It's scary and dangerous, but enthralling. It's addictive. I never fast any more.

This is the End:

It is the whole culture that is having problems with female sexuality and female power. The military guys have trouble with the fact that women protrude in ways that the uniform was not designed for. Minerva/Athena managed armor and a uniform okay, but we need to find our goddesses where we can. Diana is perhaps closest to the Twiggy-virgin body that fashion arbiters espouse; no stretch marks on our Diana. How different are the depictions of Aphrodite or Artemis from the Barbie syndrome? Bridget may be a better manifestation for us—the Celtic Triple Goddess encompasses Maiden, Mother, Crone in one lifetime. We know that Real Women come in all sizes. They also come in all Life-Stages. Barbie can be seen as an aspect of the Maiden, still unencumbered by husband and family, no Pope in sight; still open to all the possibilities that life has to offer. Give her some twining snakes and put her in a conical skirt and we recognize her. We knew her at Crete.

Okay, if we admit that Barbie and Diana and all the maiden goddesses are a manifestation of only a part of a woman's life, the next question is, How do we move on? How in this youth-obsessed culture do we endow maturing with value? The media images and the message that one can never be too thin or too rich are always with us. Autonomy is more than image, and that's what we need to convey. I really think it is a disservice to tell our live Barbie-doll-like adolescents that they are not Real Women. What, pray tell, are they? Apprentice goddesses we know, but they certainly are women, however young and confused, who should be allowed to revel in the next step.

Let's be inclusive; even skinny gals are our sisters. So are fat ones. I don't know how to bring it about, but I am of the age to still think Sisterhood is Powerful and we are all in this together. Especially those of us whose knees are giving out under the strain and who really, really need to lighten the load. Low-carbohydrate diet, anybody? Low-impact aerobics?

• *Josette, 64* •

I have been an anorexic for probably four years. I am 5 feet 9 and the lowest my weight ever got was probably 108 pounds. I am now 126 pounds. Everyday I see beautiful women everywhere and cannot help but compare myself. I was given a second opportunity to model, but I declined because I hate what the advertising industry has done to me as a woman, how it has made me feel, and how it has warped my sense of self.

I may already have a problem, and I may not be able to change the world or how people view women, but I don't have to encourage those negative stereo-types. I know how it feels to look at those women and long to be that. I refuse to make another woman long to look like me. People think that having a par-ticular figure or looking a particular way will make their lives happier. They are so wrong. They see any problems that arise out of being attractive as petty, and tell us to stop whining.

It's hard for me to get people to take me seriously as an intelligent person. I had a +4.0 GPA, but I was still judged by how I looked and was patronized by teachers and other companions, especially men. When all anybody can see is the body you inhabit, after a time, that's all you can see yourself as. I wouldn't wish this feeling on anybody.

* *Emily, 17* *

My Own True Voice

I love my body
I hate my body
They cohabit my body

Once upon a time
as a baby, I loved my body
but that was before
before my mother's voice
"No more," I said, turning
my head away in disgust.
But she held my nose
so I opened my mouth to breathe
and she shoveled in
another spoonful of food.
(healthy babies were plump, you know,
not like the sickly, dying ones
she'd seen in Europe).
So I left my body, the body I loved,
since it was no longer mine to decide,
and I lost my own true voice.

Once upon a time I loved my body,
but that was before-
before toilet training,
another torture.
If I used my diaper
I was hit.
I quickly learned
to force my immature muscles
with heroic effort
to hold it in
until it was okay
according to the world
to release them.
So I left my body, the body I loved,
since it was no longer my decision,
and I lost my own true voice

Once upon a time, I loved my body,
but that was before-
before I learned that
women were "less than"

were only good for having babies,
had no real rights, only feigned ones,
before my mother said
not to become a doctor
because then how would I
be able to have a husband
and children?
before abortions were legal,
before women were expected
to become only teachers or nurses,
before I was allowed to wear pants
to school or to work,
before I couldn't get a car loan
as a single woman unless I had
a husband,
before my Iranian-American
gynecologist refused to do my
hysterectomy unless my ex-husband
signed the consent form.
(and he had had a vasectomy
without telling me until after it was done)
I fought this time,
but lost a part of
my body, the body I loved,
since it was no longer my decision,
and I lost a part of my own true voice,
although now I knew that I had one.

Once upon a time, I loved my body,
but that was before—
before my young husband
called me a "fat pig" when I
gained 10 pounds after our
summer in Europe;
before years spent with starving
my body and regaining the weight,
before weightwatchers-richardsimmons-
janefonda-feel-the-burn-dietcenter-dietworkshop-
macrobiotics-naturalfoods-tofuburgers-dratkins-
jennycraig-dietpills-grapefruitdiet-liquiddiet
(which cost me my gall bladder) and lots of others.

before overeatersanonymous-and-years-of-therapy
for-an-eating-disorder.
I fought harder this time and struggled to learn
how to listen to my own true voice.

Once upon a time I loved my body,
but that was before—
before I learned that menstruation
was called "The Curse"
and my husband called it
"being on the rag"
before I knew that breasts
could be the "wrong size"
and I saw women all about
desperate to lose weight
and criticizing one's body
was considered natural.
before the onslaught
of advertisements
that fed off women's insecurities,
before the unstoppable greed
of the corporate world,
the patriarchal control
that tightened like a vise;
before even young men
and adolescent boys
were trained to laugh
at fat women and to mistreat them.
But now I am fighting mad
and know how to hear
my own true voice.

And now, I join in the chorus
of women everywhere
who have valiantly fought
off this epidemic,
I have learned to howl at the moon
and honor the monthly
cycle of women's lives;
I have come to know the
secrets of birth as I rebirth

myself each day, and help
others give birth to parts
of themselves;
I have learned to love
the creative juices that
flow in this woman's
body and spirit;
to write, paint, make music,
bathe this body in beauty,
colors and sounds of
celebration and joy
or grief and sadness;
I have learned to cherish
the secret powers of my
womanhood, the strengths
and burnished beauty
that is mine as I grow
older into wisdom;
I have learned to celebrate
the onset of menstruation
and have a party;
(now I call it "rag-time"
and I do a dance).
I have learned to cherish
all that is womanness, womankind,
womenfriends, women who continue
to struggle, and women everywhere.
and I reclaim my body;
I know it is mine,
and it is beautiful and
just right.
Love and hate still cohabit
this body,
but love is winning,
and I can hear
my own true voice.

• *Rosette, 54* •

131

I have parents in academia, so there was always a lot of pressure to do well academically, and in middle school I had no true friends; I always felt on the cusp of the "popular" group, always trying to fit in, but not really wanting to. My body was the one thing I felt I could control. Words that still stick in my head from those middle school years just before I developed anorexia are the comments made by boys about how hot the popular girls were because they were skinny. I wanted to be respected and revered by the boys, but mostly I wanted to be respected by myself—and when I was skinny, I had this filmy (and false) illusion of self-respect.

Finally, I was small and dainty and docile and pretty and petite and cute and slender and all those other wonderful words. Finally, I was not this big, awkward bulk getting in the way when the popular clique gathered in a huddle on the school playground. Maybe, if I could make myself as small as possible, I could fit in...smaller, smaller, smaller...I wanted people to be concerned about me, to care about me, to worry about me and love me—at first. Once I became anorexic, though, I just wanted to be left alone with my strange habits and torturous thoughts, and perfect, bony body.

• *Erica, 17* •

A beauty magazine for teenagers. Just think of the problems this could cause. In the time of a teen girl's life when they are the most vulnerable, terrified with what their friends are saying about today's fashion mistake, and thinking the zit on their nose is the size of one of Jupiter's moons, the last thing needed is a magazine screaming out to girls, "Come on, is that the best you can look?"

YM, otherwise known as *Young and Modern*, has an issue on sale right now called "Get Gorgeous!" Let's think. Are any of us completely happy with our appearance? Do we really need to have those flaws that we hope no one notices rubbed in our faces by a glossy cover featuring an actress who's had more identity crises than Michael Jackson? Is that something that's going to make me feel secure about my looks? I doubt it.

"Get Gorgeous!" features a quiz asking readers if their beauty egos are in need of a boost. What else do they expect? I am no exception to the rule, a girl in need of a confidence promotion, so I took the quiz. I fit under the category that every other girl who takes the quiz usually fits into—the middle section. I was classified as a "balanced beauty." It says, "You take care of your bod and dress up your tresses as much as the next feminina, but you're also brainy enough to know that life's way too short to spend every waking hour gazing at your own reflection." If that's the case, why do we need a magazine that shows us the "necessary" makeovers of the season and tells us a mirror-check between classes is always in order, even if it's only to apply the new guava lip gloss you picked up this weekend?

An article that caught my attention was "The Femme Features Studs Swoon For." Among those listed were earlobes, hands, shoulders, cleavage, collarbone, calves, tummy, back, and ankles. Now, in the list of the amazing feminine qualities, was a personality ever mentioned?

How about intelligence? And compassion, honesty, and respect? Nowhere to be found. Apparently those qualities that I find essential to an attractive person didn't make the cut. The morals went out the door along with the clothing of this girl scantily clad in a bikini.

We all know someone who is struggling with a weight problem. Maybe it's because of a genetic complication, or maybe just a lack of self-control. Well, "Get Gorgeous!" understands. They feel their pain. Or do they? In the article "Big Girls Don't Cry," five girls are interviewed about being overweight. But wait. Four of the five girls wear a size 12. That's a typical size, found in stores such as GAP and J. Crew.

In the pictures, they look like they could be wearing a size 8! So how is this accepting of the girls with real problems, the ones who have trouble fitting into those oh-so-comfortable desks that schools are filled with? This article is almost mocking the girls who can only fit into a size 12 in their wildest fantasies.

Now, if you still feel that you just don't make the cut, just think, a great plastic surgeon and a knife are all that's standing in your way. "The Power of Plastic" reminds us that our noses are never small enough, our cheekbones are never high enough, and our breasts are never big enough, unless of course, you're Tori Spelling and you forgot that your chest doesn't really need to be large enough to save you from drowning, they invented life jackets for that. How's that for increasing our confidence?

Wow. This magazine really makes me feel like a winner. Come on, girls. We can do better than this. In a society where women are striving for equal rights, we lower ourselves to a depth not reached by even the New York City subway system. So break out the paper shredder. The teen beauty magazines have to go. Better trash can be found in a Brooklyn dumpster.

• *Piera, 18* •

I'm not exactly sure how I came to be known as an ugly girl. My classmates were very certain of this, though. I didn't think I was all that ugly when I was a child. By junior high, though, I was taken in by the stereotypes and the magazines.

I had a subscription to *Teen* magazine. I tried very hard to fit in. I even had a pair of Guess jeans. It seemed to increase the teasing. So, in teenage rebellion, I found a look that totally annihilated fashion norms. It was called "alternative" when I was in high school. Now, they call it "goth."

This mask seemed to attract a certain crowd, and we considered it very beautiful. I was hiding my pimples, which I thought so copious and horrible that I would use bleach on my face, trying to dry them out. I covered my mirrors for years. To this day, the mirrors are relegated to the bathroom, and if I catch myself in a mirror in a department store, I still cringe at the reflection when I am naked of makeup and "figure-flattering" clothes. I spent a ton of money on cosmetics and cleansers, thinking my face was just horrible. My friends were always worried about my obsession with trying to cover all my flaws. They tried their best to convince me that my flaws were all in my head.

Those of us attracted to the goth image tend to be people who are extremely uncomfortable with their "natural" appearance. After high school, I kept this image, finding others attracted to me because of my image. I used that mask for nearly ten years. Pale makeup, blood-red lipstick (or black sometimes), thick, black Egyptian-style eyeliner, and all the black clothes you can find. Hair dye— white-blonde, black or any shade of red you want. Even now, I don't wear many colors, and when I go out, my makeup still has that stark look.

It took years for me to go out in public without my mask. It took a lot of affirmations and rituals to work on my attitude toward my face, my hair, and my body. I was comfortable with my body for a couple years. Now, I have had my first baby, and I have gone from a size 12 to a size 20. I also have stretch marks that look like zebra stripes. And my breasts went from a D to a DD, and hang lower. In all of my different sizes, my husband remains attracted to me, but I still wonder why.

• *Pyra, 26* •

Careful What You Wish For...

Sitting in the backyard playing Barbies,
under the bench, Ken doll strangely absent,
short plump legs folded Indian-Style,
dreaming of the day when I will be grown.
Pierced ears, long hair replacing my bowl cut,
eight years to go and then I'll be free.
I send Sera, my Barbie, off to work.
She is a reporter at the Tribune.
Clad in a fur coat, she walks stiffly
to the cardboard box housing "The Paper."
As Creator of Sera's world, I
hold the strings; she travels to Paris, France,
spends nights barefoot in gold lamé, dancing
in a mysterious, older man's arms.
Weekends they relax, legs rigid,
on the red plastic couch in front of a
roaring cellophane fire. He talks
of buying their dream home, already he
has given her a pink Corvette. At night
Sera wears nothing but a sheer magenta
nightie and waits for his call. Whispering
insistently, he pleads for her
patience. Just soon as the kids start school
he will leave and they will be together.
Face down on her purple pencil-case bed,
Sera's huge blue eyes fill with tears never
flowing, her smile fading yet intact.
Sitting in the backyard playing Barbies,
waiting with bated breath to be adult.

• *Victoria, 29* •

As a child in elementary school, I remember being strong. I was never wispy or waif-thin like my sister or many of the other girls at school. As I continued to grow, my body matured into womanhood at an early age. By the time I was in middle school, I had the body of an adult woman. My breasts were full, my waist trim, my hips flaring out to create the once-sought-after "hourglass figure" of so many actresses of my mother's time.

I remember being compared to Marilyn Monroe, Elizabeth Taylor, and Jane Mansfield. I was proud of that body. I never worried about my weight because I knew I was healthy. I exercised regularly, ate well, and felt good.

Then I recall my junior year in high school. My memory brings to mind an ex-boyfriend. I was fascinated by him because he was so popular, so good looking, so well built. How foolish I was. As we went for a walk one evening, he tossed me against a brick wall, and pulled out a knife. In stunned silence, I stood immobile while he raped my healthy, strong body. Within a year, I was no longer healthy or strong.

I shielded myself under layers of fat, hoping beyond hope that my "ugly exterior" would prevent any boy or man from ever forcing himself upon me again. Almost 14 years have passed, and I still hide behind a shield of excess weight. I no longer view myself as ugly because of my excess weight, although I do realize my need to regain my healthy status. My excess weight does not make me feel inferior or ugly anymore. I finally recognize my inner beauty, and my attractiveness for who I am and what I am, as opposed to how I may appear on the outside to people who judge others in that way, as I once did.

I am saddened by the overwhelming belief that thin, almost emaciated bodies are the most sought-after shape today. I long for the time when strong, healthy, "hourglass figures," were the desired shape. So many of our youth are missing out on wonderful lives as they binge, purge, and diet themselves away. What would Botticelli have to say about today's images of "beauty?" I shudder to think of his response.

• *Kelly, 29* •

The Corset

The corset of my Tante Annie
held her to the symmetry
of her youth—an immigrant
sent south to help her uncle
tend his store (I want to shelter her—
the broken English, the strangeness
of a Jew, of a body at fourteen).
She was alone. Four boys ganged her.
For one year she had to stay in an asylum.

No one told. North, she met her husband
whose artistic, fluent ways enabled her
to ripple like a fountain. But not so fast—

first she grew fat, so that each morning,
bone by bone, a corset laced the chaos
to its parts: full breasts, slim waist,
round hips: a figure eight to match my age
those summer nights I shared her room
and saw the miracle, how, stay by stay,
lace by lace, she loosened the reined flesh
and sent it tumbling—ahhh a machaiah!
fold by fold, sigh by sigh, the drench of it
so delicious I told everyone
when I was grown I wanted fat
like hers, vast and operatic.

• *Myra, 67* •

When I was a little girl I was taught that being fat was bad and caused nothing but pain. As I naturally bloomed into a curvy, voluptuous body in my early teens, the fear of fat developed into an eating disorder, anorexia. I have since then lost eight years of life.

I have not led a normal life because I've been struggling with this horrid disease. I've lost so many wonderful opportunities: studying abroad, talented riding career, horses, friends, college, money, joy, life, happiness, social activity, and dreams. I almost died last month and was put in treatment.

There I gained a lot of weight, but I was still underweight for my size. That weight gain made me suicidal although it was good for my health; I could not see that—all I saw was a gross body, and I felt deep hatred for myself. Now I struggle to keep this weight on, but I'm on a path of eating less. I see other woman and marvel at the beauty of their bodies no matter what size they are. I see beauty in every woman, but not myself. I pray to find peace with my body at a healthy size, even if it's bigger than what I'd like. I pray to recover because I'm dying now. I pray to see the start of body acceptance, real-sized women in ads, the return of high esteem to women of every size, and the glory that should be felt in every woman for having a beautiful creative body in every shape, form, condition, and size. I thank you more than you'll ever know for this project. This is what we need more of. God bless you!

• *Sarah, 21* •

Finally I Just Gave Up

It became too much to keep up
the pretense of my desirability—
the empty bed, the silent meals
his eyes that saw through me
with no flicker of recognition
Finally I just gave up and became fat
letting the lard build up around me in layers
letting it roll into ridges around my hips
and bulge along the cross-your-heart
of my triple D cups.

Feeling myself slip into invisibility
I ate more, stuffing myself with
meat, potatoes, corn and rice
solid food with substance,
heavy, real weight, working with gravity
to keep me on the ground
keep me around.

I became less visible than ever;
people averted their faces not daring
to look me in the eye but staring
after me in horrid fascination.
Even the clerk at Safeway,
taught to befriend each customer,
gazed straight at her machine and mumbled,
thrusting the receipt toward my hand
without touching me,
saving herself for the next shopper,
greeting them with rolled eyes and relief,
freed from brief alliance with a freak.

It took ten months of starving
but the weight dropped off.
With the help of Ex-lax and diet pills
I changed dress sizes as fast as a baby
rattlesnake sheds skins—
eighteen, fourteen, twelve, ten
eight, six
once I even squeezed into
a slinky black four of an evening dress.

It was vintage clothes I wanted
with pinched waists, low-cut necks
and full flared skirts.
I hungered after tube tops,
tight, crotch-pinching jeans
and fluffy cashmere sweaters.

Now I was visible with a vengeance.
The same man who once ran into my
heel with a grocery cart because he
didn't see me, asked me to advise
him on the relative merits of
Wheaties and Post Toasties.
He failed to recognize me.
So did Sharon, who dropped me
when I topped two hundred,
then stopped me in the mall last week
to wonder why I looked familiar.

I have become president of the PTA
and the flower coordinator at St. John's Episcopal.
My daughter and only five other little girls
got invited to Jane Jackson's birthday party—
last year Mrs. Jackson refused to let Jane
attend a sleep-over at our house.

He still doesn't want me—
in fact things are worse than ever.
Now that he can see me again
he screens my calls, accuses me of infidelity
rages at my makeup, clothes, high-faluting airs.
He's jealous like a dog in a manger
afraid of losing something he refuses to possess.
So last night after he turned away from me again
I walked through the dark house into the kitchen
and ate the Ding-Dongs out of Katie's lunchbox.

• *Chris, 47* •

At 46, I am in Vanity's gray area between pride and self-loathing. I have the urge to lie about my age, but then I am truthful, hoping for the "Wow, you look great!" response. One day it became evident that I should forego that hope, and think honestly about getting older.

My husband Len, a physician, does not alarm easily. I am the mother of two sons, 20 and 16. I am also a hypochondriac. Having admitted this, you will understand my hysteria when one morning while dressing Len asked me to lie on the bed so he could examine something. I have not been pregnant for many years. Yet there was a protuberant nature to my upper abdomen.

"What?" I swallowed hard.

"It's bulging. Feels like a hernia. I'm calling Dr. Dotoo Much. Plastic surgeon. He knows bellies."

Professional courtesy is not all it's cracked up to be. I got in to see him that afternoon. Entering his reception area, I took a seat in the dimmed light. A romantic glow was produced from the laminated brochures of abdominal surgery. The outlined diagram in drawing #1 detailed the surgical "correction" — indicated an incision of the entire lower quadrant of the torso; picture #2 illustrated some major seam work to put the old girl back together. End pix: Perfection.

A young woman came into the waiting room from behind the locked door and invited me in. After taking a brief history she opened a drawer and removed something plastic. "Here," she offered, and handed me a tiny bag that held a pair of disposable panties. I thought for a moment I was getting a souvenir.

I was instructed to change into my new undies and to stand in front of the white wall for photos. "The doctor will look at these before he sees you," the young woman said. Then she had me turn to the side so she could get a good shot of my protrusive condition.

I was conscious of my ambivalent feelings about my body, that One: I was a perfectly normal and healthy specimen of womanhood, and that Two: I was grossly disfigured. Subconsciously I must have believed this doctor would tell me the former was correct, judging from my utter shock at what followed.

When Dr. Dotoo Much appeared in my exam room, I was fully draped in a white sheet. We smiled politely, and then he told me to stand in front of him without the sheet. Okay, I thought, this is just another doctor seeing me undressed. As a certified hypochondriac, this happens to me often. I am fairly certain though, that this disposable panty thing was a first.

A tape measure was stretched up over my torso as the doctor recited numbers in centimeters to the nurse. He asked me to lie down, and palpated my abdomen in the same manner as my husband had. "The good news is twofold. You don't need liposuction [I don't recall asking this] but I can fix this condition. It's called rectus diastases."

Decision, I could cry or wait for him to speak in English. My silence prompted him to continue. "It's from your pregnancies," he said. "You tore the muscle, damaged it so thoroughly, so permanently, that it forces this bulge." He poked at it. "More or less a herniation." He again pressed into me with his three middle fingers. "But I can fix it," he repeated. "I can make you look twenty again. You could wear a bikini!" Then he added that the corrective procedure is called an abdominoplasty.

Luckily, I had done my reading in the waiting room and I knew what that word meant. "You mean you want to cut me open? So what you're saying is that you want to cut me open so I can wear a bikini?"

"Look," he said sitting back on his stool, "I am an artist. I'm telling you how I see it as an artist." At once it crystallized for me—it was time to get out of this gallery. I stood up in my panties and wrapped the sheet around me.

Rising from his stool, he and nurse I'am Soyoung swung out of the room. I thought I saw a cape trailing behind him.

Then I remembered those pregnancies that ripped my muscles apart. The ones I had taken years worth of Pergonal to have. Posing in the door mirror, pushing in on my slight protrusion, I felt a tiny bony foot still sticking me from under my rib. I smiled, recalling how my husband would feel it, trying as parents do, to gently nudge, guide our children into their natural, comfortable selves. Pride restored.

• *Beth, 46* •

143

I am a soon-to-be 37-year-old mother of two. I stand approximately 5 feet 8 and weigh around 150 pounds. I was always one of the tallest girls in my class while growing up, and was constantly teased about it. At that time I looked at my height as a "bad thing" and always wished I were shorter. Then, around age 11 to 12, I started developing breasts, and was again teased when the boys could see my training bra lines through my shirt. It was a devastating blow to an overly sensitive girl whose self-confidence had already taken a plunge. After that, I tried to hide my growing breasts just to spare anymore embarrassment. In junior high, it became apparent to me that breasts weren't all that bad and that the boys now had an altogether different view of them. Now it was "the bigger the better." My breasts then became a commodity that seemed to have a value separate from the rest of me. And they could be used in exactly such a way. Also, my height didn't seem to bother anyone either, so naturally I accepted it also.

In high school I was even more accepted/acceptable. My lean, young body was stared at and commented upon as if it were right out of a museum. Surprisingly, this only gave me an even more unfulfilled kind of feeling about myself. My self-confidence was still at a low. Why? Looking back now, I realize that young girls have little or no direction, guidance, or nurturing in learning what they *really* are and discovering the beauty in the female body. We, as females, accept ourselves only when the outside world gives its okay, and we waste time starving ourselves and molding ourselves into something that is acceptable to others, truly denying ourselves the precious time we should have getting in touch with the truth, the perfect beauty of what we are.

As I grew older, I continued to use my body as a means of getting what I wanted or needed in life. It was easy as long as I fit the part. One day I woke up and realized my body wasn't what it used to be. I was heavier, older, slower, less appealing to the world. I felt angry and empty. At around 30 years old, I decided to "rebuild" my body. I went to the gym everyday, practically stopped eating altogether, got a fake tan and a new hairdo.

Ironically, with every accepting stare and whistle, I felt empty. "Is this all there is?" I thought to myself. In a way, I resented myself for carrying the sins of the world in my body. I despised myself for not being true to myself. Who was I, after all this time? What was I? I didn't know a thing about myself. I felt like a fake—like nothing more than just a body.

Now, at 36, I've decided that enough is enough. I am, and all women are, more than just bodies. I'm sick of suppressing what I am to satisfy what some people perceive as acceptable. Now I'm taking care of the *real* me and as a result, I'm

144

feeling alright with my body! It seems to go hand-in-hand, but it had to start with a part of me that I can't touch or see, a part of me that is hard to put into words. Yes, at one point, if you had asked me "if there were one thing you could change about your body, would you change anything and what would it be?" I'd surely have had a list for you. But now, I'm finally comfortable with my body and I wouldn't change a thing. Besides, if I changed anything, anything at all— it just wouldn't be me anymore, and I like who and what I am now. Now that I know.

• *Theresa, 36* •

I am not sure if my story is unique, but it is how I saw the world and how I thought the world saw me. I spent my childhood in a large family of mostly brown people. Only one had the same skin as me, and we two out of the 15 in the family had to cling tight to each other. She was the mother who had a team of 13 children, and I the girl who never saw her rest. My mother was the strongest person in the house because she had to be. As a child I thought that this was because she was bigger than us, but when I was a teenager my father told me the reason for my mother's strength was her color. That she had to be extra good at everything she did because if you were as dark as her there was no other way to deal.

In this world there are two kinds of people: those who do because they want to, and those who do because they must. When my mom grew up it was a case of if you are dark you will work like a dog in the street for a scrap, but if you are light (and therefore pretty) you can relax.

She always said to me that I had to be better than anything or anybody if I was going to have anything. This she knew based on the fact that I was not an exceptional beauty, and my skin, though not as dark as hers, was still too black to be brown.

It was really weird growing up after that, knowing that by just a mistake of DNA I would have to work instead of till 5 p.m. each day, I would be up till almost dawn. That instead of relaxing in the sun at the beach (Atlantic City), I would be putting stuff out and getting stuff ready; that instead of seeing that the best time of life is now, I would be praying for the time when I would be able to rest.

My mother died in 1997, and up to that time I saw not one day that she didn't try to be more than just good! She always tried to be perfect. The fact that all of her kids were well wasn't enough. The fact that the house was clean wasn't enough. She had to make everything shine. What my mother taught me by not ever resting, never letting good enough be good enough, was that no matter how hard you try color will and does matter. Being dark means that you were fired longer than the rest, that you are stronger and you must be that way or you will die. Being darker means that you have something to prove because the world wants proof. Being darker means that you will die before you will rest because you can't rest.

I fight this everyday. I try to convince myself that good enough is, and I try to allow myself to rest. But that itch (one more thing to do) keeps at you until you are on your feet again. Maybe someday my prayer, her prayer, will be answered:

that you have to be better, stronger, smarter just to be like the others will be forgotten. I will sit down on a beach blanket or maybe just calm down, and I will rest. I won't have to die just to get a little peace of mind, I won't have to prove to the world or myself that I am good enough, that it is clean enough, because I will just know it is. Right now all I can say is that having a point to make has made me successful and lonely, to some rich, and to myself, one of the saddest, poorest people in the world.

• Adrienne, 31 •

My Black Skin was a sign of ugliness. I did not realize how much I hated myself until I started to think about my journey, my painful journey. When I was growing up, my older sister was "the light one" and I was called "the dark one." There are five girls in my family and we are different shades, different colors. I knew early that light was good and dark was bad. It was as if you could see light/white people, but dark-skinned folk were invisible.

I remember wearing a straight wig in the fourth grade because I did not want to comb my hair. I would sit outside in my aunt's yard and swing my wig hair about my head as if the wind was blowing my hair. That is the closest I've come to being white. My skin color has gotten in the way. Internalized racism has been my constant companion. When I go shopping it is there, when I want to educate myself, when I apply for a job or move up in my field, when I want to rent an apartment or buy a home, and when I take my children to school...racism or internalized racism is always there.

I know that there are places in this world where the color of your skin does not matter, but not in my world. It matters, it matters!!! No matter how pretty I may be, my little-girl self is reminded that I am the dark one. My body was not an issue until I got older. Big hips and a big butt was a good thing in my community. I had neither. So I ate an extra helping of eggs and bacon so that I could gain weight. When my third child was born, I struggled with my size. I was fat. I was depressed, and I got fatter. Now I go up and down. I eat to feel good and I hate my body especially when I cannot fit into my clothes. I will be 40 in December, and all I want is to accept my Black Skin, my body, all of me.

I do not want to be the size of a model. I do not want my culture or the dominant culture to dictate to me what I should look like. I have been living like a yo-yo. I'm not light enough, I'm too dark, too fat, too skinny...I'm not enough. I have spent so much time on my weight, on my body. I thought if only I looked like this, I will be right, acceptable. When I turn 40, all I want is to be at peace with myself, to love the skin that God blessed me with, to love my body as my most cherished gift, to accept all of me. I'd like to wake up without internalized racism. I'd like to wake up and be free.

• *Evette, 39* •

For the first time in my life, at 33 years old, the self-consciousness I have had with me ever since I can remember has begun to fade. When I walked out of the optical department of Sears last August, wearing my very first pair of glasses, I suddenly felt like I had permission to be an intelligent girl, instead of a sexual object. I know it sounds strange, but my glasses have given me back my true self. My glasses are a barrier, a protection of sorts.

It is not that being an intelligent girl has not been an option. I went to college and to graduate school. It is just that, as I pursued my education, I fought the inner demon of having to be the perfect woman—the provocative, sexy woman I saw staring out at me from the magazines I've seen since I was a child.

On the societal spectrum, the body I have lived in these 33 years has fallen into the physically acceptable range—on the "anorexic" end of the scale. As a young girl, I blamed my body for being the source of pain and the source of much unwanted attention. With the onset of early menstruation (at age 11), and early breast development, I felt rushed into puberty and the attendant influx of male attention.

A rape when I was 14 years old and an escalation of craziness in the men I chose to date led me into the arms of my first girlfriend. After the rape, I linked my body to impending violence. Now, 20 years later, after much soul-searching, I find myself embarking on a new cycle of life, enjoying my first year of marriage with my husband.

The peace I have found with my past and with my body grew out of a rich web of experiences gained by going to college. The story I want to tell you is one that to this day reminds me that my body, any way it changes, is uniquely and beautifully my own to enjoy.

During my undergraduate studies, I took an "Introduction to Women's Studies" class, led by a silver-haired renegade who was on the run from the administration. Getting an A in this teacher's class involved demonstrating at the state capital in Sacramento, campaigning for Roe v. Wade, and the possibility of going to jail for any number of rebellious acts, like covering the sidewalks of the campus with graffiti (washable chalk—we had a conscience) after the story broke in the news in the late 1980s about the man who opened fire on 13 women students in Montreal.

But my favorite "act" was one for which we targeted a plastic surgeon coming to campus to discuss breast augmentation. While our teacher could not accompany us, having been reprimanded by the Dean's Office for a previous mission involving a date rape at one of the fraternities, she did help us plan out the demonstration.

Twenty of us entered the lecture hall where the plastic surgeon was scheduled to speak. We sat politely through the young doctor's talk as he presented slides of Raquel Welch. He used a long pointer to point out the difference between Raquel, and then "subject A," who had "imperfect breasts."

"See here," he said, "this breast slopes down a good one-fourth of an inch, like the end of a semi." He tapped on the offending breast, which looked entirely normal to me. He flicked up the next series of slides. Intermingled with photos of the breasts of model after model were slides of women with "uneven, less than ideal" breasts.

"The beauty of surgery is that anything can be fixed," the doctor continued. "There is no reason you can't have perfect breasts." Toward the end of the doctor's presentation, a woman raised her hand.

"I have had severe back pain for most of my life because of the reverse. I mean, my breasts are too large."

"I'm sorry," the doctor said, shaking his head, "I have only been trained in augmentations."

When the lights came up after the slide show, twenty of us rose and took off our shirts. We stood, breasts exposed in the cool air of the room. I remember the row of naked backs in front of me, and seeing out of the corner of my eye the row of breasts on either side of me. How some of us stood straight, proud, some of us with shoulders curved in, shy. The shocked expressions on the faces of the handful of women still seated.

My friend Karen read our statement: "Variety is beauty. There is no such thing as the perfect breast. We believe women's breasts are meant for, One: a woman's pleasure (her own), and Two: to feed her children. We don't believe the scalpel is the answer to happiness." Three of us in the middle row had taken an eyebrow pencil to our chests. There we had traced the letters: VARIETY IS BEAUTY, one word apiece.

The doctor stood juggling his example silicon implants from palm to palm. We left the room quietly at his request. Several moments later, as we pulled our sweatshirts back on, a woman joined us in the parking lot.

"I honestly didn't know women's bodies were so different until I looked around

150

at all of you," she said, crying. "You all look beautiful to me. I didn't know breasts came in so many different sizes…" We circled around her. She continued, "I see that I'm not so different. There's nothing wrong with me. I can't thank you enough. I'm calling off my surgery."

I know that some women choose to surgically alter their bodies. I am not saying that breast augmentation is wrong. It is not the choice I would make, but I believe we all have the right to make those kinds of decisions for ourselves. But sometimes we don't know we have choices, just like the woman who followed us out to the parking lot. She had perhaps been, like many of us, deluged under the images we find in popular culture of the perfect woman. And bought the attendant myth, that "perfect body" means "perfect life."

I work every day at staying inside of my own body, where I can experience my life, instead of standing outside of my body judging it as others would judge it—as too thin, too fat, too sexy, not sexy enough.

Don't get me wrong—I know I can wear glasses and be sexy, if I desire. The key is that I get to experience the full range of human emotions from inside this body I was born with. And that I choose who gets to touch this body!

• *Tania, 33* •

151

Dancing Home

My body is a small thing.
The space it occupies
has not always been home.
I was big at the mighty age of 6
but shrinking at 12
quaking at 18
starved for a breath at 21.

The little-girl me twirled in skirts that flared
and worshiped the solidity of earth under her feet.
I have followed her back to that first bliss.

I know now my body contains oceans.
I have remembered at last
that the space it dances in—
wild, sweet spirit—
welcomes beyond measure.

• *Shawndra, 33* •

What they don't tell you, when they are pushing you to be skinny and sexy and feminine, is that being a little bit heavy makes you feel substantial, and when you feel substantial, you feel like people can't push you around anymore, and when you feel like people can't push you around anymore, you find it a lot easier to stand up for yourself and stand your ground, literally as well as symbolically.

I want to lose weight so I can feel fit and attractive. I don't ever want to lose the sense that my real physical power is not sexual, but something deeper that I don't even have the words to name. I want to love my body the way it is, but it's so hard not to look in the mirror and see me, with extra stuff added, rather than accepting the fat as part of me today. I think I feel best when I feel strong and safe and happy, whatever my size, because the times I've been skinniest have been when I was under the most emotional stress and wasn't eating well and was running on adrenaline, and I don't want to live in that craziness.

I have known moments of feeling really good about myself and my body, and I wish I could have a lot more of them. I love other women who are bigger than I am, but I always apply the mean double standard to myself. I am growing and changing so much, but this way I view myself hasn't much changed. Yet. I'm doing yoga and Tae-bo and therapy and 12-step work, and I will find greater happiness and health with my body, and I am finding peace with who I am. I love the feeling of being strong, and watching other women being strong.

• *Holly, 32* •

Soap Sculpture

Girl Scout pocket knives
Were green plastic anomalies

Sheathing a blade
meant only for whittling

I attempted carving with a kitchen knife.
All I got was rough points on sticks.

I rendered bars of Ivory to crumbs,
Not delicate birds.

Convinced of its purpose,
I desired that knife.

I hoped to turn unwieldy mass
Into beauty.

My body rounded itself new and difficult.
The boys were not kind.

Only one classmate had gone before me
into womanhood.

It was a rude time for transformation,
adjusting to female.

While Twiggy's manager
whittled her boyish for the camera.

I wanted to pare my thighs and hips
Into long, thin sticks.

I dreamed of planing my torso flat.
I prayed for a firmer chisel

to finish
what the lathe of heaven left undone.

• *Georgia, 46* •

Bathing

This morning I helped my mother take a bath because she is so full of pain it's hard for her to climb in and out of the tub or even hold the hand shower nozzle. They think it's degenerative arthritis in her spine or cancer, but all I know is she has wasted away to nothing and gets tired out just hobbling across her bedroom with a walker. The pain in her right leg is so bad she sleeps every night with a big bag of ice in her groin. One leg is always on fire and the other one icy cold. It's been three weeks since she has taught her dance classes, and even longer since she's danced herself. All those years of grace and movement now come to a standstill.

My mother was never very big, but now I don't think she weighs even 100 pounds. Pulling the oversized flannel pajama top up over her head before the bath, I saw that her flesh hung in folds, more like drapes than anything that could hold a body together. Her skin was smooth all over, and luminescent, like the inside of an oyster shell. When I touched her the softness filled me with grief. She looked up at me shyly, and said: "Imagine having to give your mother a bath." I thought her beautiful there in the tub, shivering, and scrubbing under her arms, while I let the hot water pour over her shoulders and back and down her chest, all bones and knobs. She let out a sigh that ended in a groan, and told me it felt good to have the hot water run over her skin.

She squirted a small amount of shampoo into her palm and rubbed it in her hair, all the while enjoying the running water, I could tell. When she'd lathered it up into a sudsy bouffant, she dropped her hands in the water and bowed her head as I trained the spray onto her head. She wallowed in the heat and smoothness of the running water, and when her hair was thoroughly rinsed, she lathered it up again.

When she was finished, we waited in silence while all the water ran out. I couldn't take my eyes off her. How frail she looked! But I knew there was great strength in those thin arms, and that her flattened, ribby chest was full of a heart of gold. Her breasts were flat to her chest, only the nipples jutting out, and I admired her from my seat on the john.

I helped her out of the tub, and as she walked naked the short distance from bathroom to bedroom, I held my arms out behind, in a semi-circle around her. More like a halo of protection than any tangible support, for she was managing fine with the walker. From behind I saw the shape of her: square shoulders, narrow back, hip bones flaring out, thighs in proportion to the rest of her tiny body, her poor swollen feet shaped so like mine. I reached out and touched her protruding spine as she hobbled across the sill of her bedroom door. She paused a moment before sitting down, and I let my hand rest where it was.

Then she kind of swirled around in one deft movement that planted her square on the bed, the dancer making art out of the hard work of movement. She let go of the walker and let out a sigh. I placed a clean cotton pajama top across her shoulders while I did her hair, more for warmth than modesty. My mother has never been ashamed of her naked body, and she wasn't now.

As I toweled off her hair, we talked about her upcoming doctor appointment. I combed out the damp hair and twisted it into tight pin-curls, as she'd asked me to do. Make them nice and tight, she said, so they'll last. She wanted to look good at the doctor's.

Later that afternoon, after a meandering walk through the neighborhood to think, I came home flushed and hot, and ran myself a bath. Standing naked by the side of the tub while it filled, I looked down at my own voluptuous body, enjoying as always the sight of so much flesh, the mounds and hollows, full breasts, the flare and curve of my hips, sinewy thighs, large nicely-shaped feet, rounded mountain of belly, and the way hair grows all over me, in soft blond down as well as dark curly tufts. I loved my strong mature body more than ever at that moment, my mother's gift to me. My skin covered in a sheen of sweat, redolent of sex and underarms, body aching and tired from the day's efforts. Outside, the air was full of cicada song, a dry breeze swelled out the curtains at the window, as if someone, some other woman, was out there trying to come in, pressing her body into the room, wanting to be seen, and touched, and loved, and wept over.

• *Teresa, 52* •

As a child, I was a picky eater and unusually thin. I wasn't trying to be thin, but since I was, this became a big part of my identity. In the mid-1960s, I was the ideal clotheshorse for the radical mod clothes: 5 feet 5 inches and 100 pounds. Other girls were jealous of my thinness, and I began to watch my diet in order to protect my status.

At 18, the normal poundage of womanhood began to creep on, and I was miserable. I began years of intermittent masochistic dieting, even though no one would have called me fat. Everyone in the dorm dieted, it was normal. Last year I attempted to write about how well I had recovered from my eating/ body image disorder. I made several false starts but just couldn't pull it together. Months later I realized: I haven't recovered. I still experience flare-ups of feeling fat and wanting to be thinner above all else. Fortunately, my healthy appetite keeps me from doing much damage.

This fall I bought six new pairs of pants in my new size, 10. I had been packing myself into size 8 for years! I continue to recover on a daily basis, with the help of positive messages such as the ones from your group. I do blame the mass media, especially fashion magazines and television, for the national obsession with size.

No, not many people would call me fat, but I can think of some who would: anorexics. Recruiters from modeling agencies.

And on a bad day, myself.

My personal conclusion about my eating-body-image-obsession is this: if I am wrapped up in worrying about food, size, and weight, I don't have to worry about living the rest of my life. My best advice is: get rid of that scale!

• *Kelly, 48* •

Prayer To Blessed Fat

It's been so long since I was held
felt like a woman at all
this body great with children once
is now used, not fertile,
but fertile still for other reasons

rolls of flesh, I say to you:
"you have served me well,
protected me when I needed to feel safe,
kept me from others,
a barrier, insulation,
until I could find other ways to feel safe.
now I don't need you so much anymore
It's time for you to go
Goodbye" I say, "and thank you
ever so much."

and when I couldn't face being a woman
when men's attention frightened me too much
this body became round and amorphous
to defend me, losing its female curves
to blessed fat.
"Thank you" I say, "for your protection
but I think I can handle things now on my own.
It's time for you to go—
I'm scared to see you leave
but now is the time for a new beginning
the time is ripe for a new love
for my flesh to be opened in close embrace
to find space within space for love
the place where I'll feel
like a woman again.
Goodbye" I say, "and thank you
ever so much."

I know it will happen
I can feel the transformation
I'm ready for the energy to flow into my life
opened to love, no longer so afraid.
Grand is the feeling, no, miraculous.
I thought it would never come;

"Thank you" I say, "for this healing, this renewal,
life is returning to this once-dead body
and my spirit is lifted into new joy."

• *Rosette, 54* •

When I was pregnant at 24 years, I began to feel the power of the life-force given to me as a woman. Through the years of sexual abuse and rape, I had never realized the power of my own body. Now as a massage therapist, I feel the power in the "large" women patients I am honored to treat.

It becomes my goal with these beautiful goddesses to allow them to take up all the space they deserve and to delight in it through the power of touch by another. My daughter, unknowingly, as an unborn child, gave me the gift of touch which transformed me into a woman of power. She lives the life of the goddess in the form of the maiden. Life is good. Take up all the space you can and absorb it all!

• *Lauri, 39* •

Growing up, I might have said that my self-image and self-esteem were definitely affected by my size, shape, and race. But truthfully, we know now that these characteristics of mine did not affect my self-esteem, but rather that society's views and treatment of them did, and my acceptance of them did as well.

Looking back, though, as a child it would be pretty hard to escape the influences and harsh judgments of my surroundings. I'm not entirely sure when I lost my naïveté and innocence when it came to my views of my body—when I was able to loll about in a homemade string bikini, fingers and toes digging into the sand, with absolutely no thoughts as to whether I had a "correct" shape.

I do recall when I was about 6 or so, my father calling my brother and sister (who at the time where experiencing natural fluctuations in body weight) "potatoes." "Why can't you be more like your sister?" he would proclaim, pointing at my stringbean body. Then he would make us run for miles each Sunday, my brother and him off in the distance, my sister trailing, and I, blocks behind, terrified of the dogs following me and of the loneliness I felt. I know this set me up for feeling that being fat was unacceptable, unlovable, bad. Watching my mother only cemented these feelings—she was constantly dieting, eating soup while the rest of us ate dinner and she watched on. She fed us bountifully, getting vicarious pleasure in our eating.

Later, at school, only the popular, thin, blond, blue-eyed girls made it onto the cheerleading team, got their hair pulled by boys. I felt like a lump in comparison, with my Latin features and thick thighs. Soon enough, around the age of 13, I began to diet. I experimented with diet pills (which made me shake like the dickens) and a never-ending stream of fad diets. I was a virtual dictionary of different diet plans: Atkins Diet Revolution, the Mayo Clinic Diet, the Beverly Hills Diet, the 3-day Stewardess diet, et al. I did join my track and cross-country teams, but primarily to lose weight. I don't know how I found the energy to run 5 miles with just an apple sitting in my stomach from lunchtime.

Then, around age 17 (at 5 feet 8 inches and 115 pounds), I found out that a friend of mine would go home each day, eat about three bowls of cereal, and throw it up. Rather than being disgusted, I thought, wow—what a great idea! That was the beginning of the end. I eventually got up to throwing up 5 times a day, eating whole pies, bags of cookies and anything else I could get my hands on. Amazingly, during this time, I managed to get a degree in Architecture from UC Berkeley. But all through college, my relationships with other people were secondary to my secret relationship with food, and I was miserable.

Today, I've not been a bulimic for over five years, and I have a fairly healthy attitude toward food. I deeply regret the years I lost by focusing on my body rather than on developing my mind, relationships, soul, and life—and yet I still find myself beating myself up over my body's shape. "I'm so fat...I'm so ugly...if only I had model-like thighs." What a waste! It makes me so furious! The crazy thing is that I know that other people don't view me that way. They're always commenting on how thin I am and how great I look. So, why can't I love my body which has served me so well? After all I've done to it, it's still so healthy, it's still capable of running up stairs, lifting huge suitcases, breathing, healing, loving. I know I should love it in return and that, if I actually did, it would finally become what I want it to be. More than that, I know that it is just part of who I am and that I am so much more than just my body parts—I have a mind, a spirit, and energy to change the world. Luckily, I know. I'm a bit closer to being whole every day.

• *Pamela, 32* •

War Paint

Every morning
I get up
and get ready for war

Every morning
I get up
and put on my armor

To protect me
Not my body,
My soul.

Every morning
I get up
To apply my war paint

Some on the eyes
A little on the cheeks
And some lipstick

Every day
I go out
And I fight my war
Makeup, high heels, and all.

• *Lily, 13* •

Middle
Age(ing)

I mind
my waist
    I mind
as I watch it expand
hips grow out
thighs become twice their usual size
the scale shoots up
    in disbelief
I hear numbers
never before associated with me
    weight
    blood pressure
    measurements
    age
try to shop in a large size store
but I am too small
go to a department store
but clothes don't quite fit
I am at an in-between time
last time this happened
I was 13
    not quite adult
    not quite kid
with a body I didn't understand
    or like
yet I came to love it
to feel good in my clothes
develop my own
sense of style
now
that slips away
I don't know my style
colors I wore
with my dark brown hair
    look terrible now with gray
some old jewelry ridiculous
some sweaters too baggy
some old baggy sweaters
    now too tight

I am growing
   growing old
      growing large
         growing humble
now
I understand
that what is inside
and what is outside
may not always match

• *Mary, 57* •

Enough of This

This is for the woman who looked up from the bowl to see a reflection in the mirror she did not recognize as her own. This is for the starving girls with the signature knuckles who do not know where to turn to feed their spirit. This is for the woman I was until I said "enough of this."

This is for my mother, who could not see, nor hear, my suffering. This is for my grandmother, who would never fathom a generation of women who simply pushed their food around the plate. This is for my sisters and cousins and friends, none of whom knew this would be the cost of beauty.

This is for my teachers who guided my mind, not knowing how I hated my body. This is for all the girls in my kindergarten class, neatly arranged in corn-cob rows of even wooden chairs smiling at the camera; a camera that would later imprison them with an image of beauty they could not achieve without chronic dieting. This is for those precious little girls who still eat to grow and have not yet learned to count and measure and carry tiny scales with them to the salad bar.

Most of all, this is for my daughter, a daughter who is not even born. A daughter I would comfort, tasting the tears off her cheek when one day she, too, learns that she is not pretty enough, she is not perfect enough, she is not anything enough—simply not enough. This is for the tears I will cry with her because I have no words to feed the empty place in her that will never understand that she absolutely IS just enough.

• Maggie, 37 •

166

Give Them This

Look, I've told you before about hips,
about the early goddess statues
that celebrate curves and rounding flesh:
prosperity, fertility, lust.

Ah Lust

Give them something to run their hands
down, I say. Give them a pawful, a palmful,
something to wrap their fingers around.

Give them melon flesh and musk scent.
Give them skin soft as watercolor
and feet like the petals of magnolia.

Give them river-hands and tumulus of belly
so the hand slides without a hitch of bone.
It's not rib and hip joint they want to stroke,

not reef or rockbound coast.
They want ocean.
They want land that yields.

They want to feel
they've gotten hold of something:
give them mountains.

Let them climb hand over hand
across the foothills
from base camp to base camp.

Let them reach the top, the apex,
the acme of the world, and without rest
start down the other side.

Keep them traveling the continents.
Let them taste the inlets, the outcrops.
Let them tongue salt and cinnamon.

Let them lap it, and lip it,
and enter, and divide, and explode,
and submit:

and now,
and now if we are willing,
let them rest.

• *Carolyn, 63* •

167

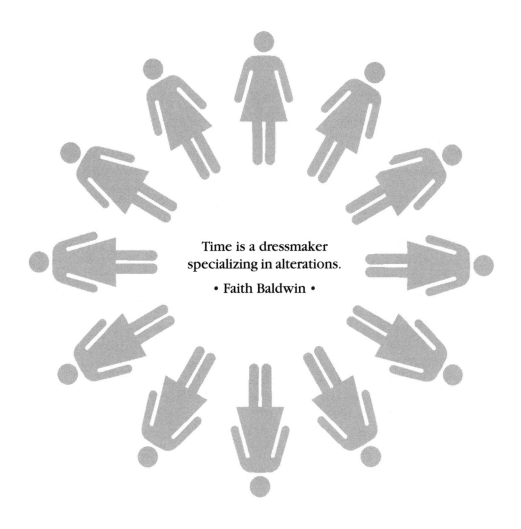

Time is a dressmaker
specializing in alterations.

• Faith Baldwin •

AN OPEN LETTER FROM A PSYCHOTHERAPIST

One of the glaring realities illustrated by these stories is how women are disempowered as much by the media as our own self-talk. We have two forces working against us in this battle for self-love—one comes from the barrage of media messages that say we're not beautiful, not acceptable if we don't fit into this rigid and narrow definition of beauty. The other is our own internal communication, the ways we berate ourselves for how we look, constantly criticizing ourselves for not being thin enough, proportioned properly, wrinkle-free, cellulite free, and on and on. Both of these forces—the internal and external—have direct consequences on our health and well-being and it is my hope here to broaden our understanding of the nature and power of these forces.

Mind Over Media

- A $40 billion a year diet industry
- A $20 billion a year cosmetic industry
- An average exposure to 400 to 600 ads a day
  —1 out of 11 pertaining to "beauty" or beauty-related products

Let's take a look first at the media. There is a $40 billion a year diet industry and a $20 billion cosmetic industry that in many cases has played to our insecurities about how we look. As a change agent, I'm not against people deciding that they don't want to carry extra weight because it's not healthy for them, or using cosmetics because they love to, but a lot of the dollars behind those industries are driven by self-hate and fear, not by self-love, fun, or curiosity. And many of those products are sold with the promise that if we use them, our lives will be better, we'll have better relationships, better sex, more success.

If we make our purchases based on fears like "I won't get a date if I don't look as good as so-and-so…If I'm not thinner, no man will ever want me…If I don't get rid of these wrinkles, my husband will run off with a younger woman," we're being driven by insecurity, buying everything we can get our hands on that promises *some* kind of security. The advertisers know how to capitalize on our fears.

They associate their product with an outcome they know we want and over and over we're reminded of that outcome when we look at the ad. And we are highly susceptible to the repetitious and seductive imagery in ads.

Here's an example of the power of advertising. See how many products or companies you can identify from these slogans:

- Reach out and touch someone.

- It keeps going and going and going.
- Have you driven a _____ lately.
- We bring good things to life.
- Sometimes you feel like a nut, sometimes you don't.
- Let your fingers do the walking.
- How do you spell relief?
- Just do it.
- Pop, pop, fizz, fizz, oh what a relief it is.
- Just for the taste of it, Diet _____ .
- Give us a week and we'll take off the weight.
- Don't leave home without it.
- Fly the friendly skies of _____ .

You probably know most of these because you have those slogans in your head from years ago, and *not* because you memorized them. It's because you heard the same message over and over. It seeps in whether we're aware of it or not.

So if you consider that the average person sees between 400 and 600 ads a day, and 1 out of 11 of those pertain to beauty and are making some inappropriate promises to us—"If you look like this, you're going to have a better life"—then you see how susceptible we are to *others'* version of what is beautiful and acceptable. Others, I might add, who are profiting from our insecurity and spending billions to increase it.

When we try to live up to the versions of beautiful portrayed by reed-thin models and airbrushed photographs, it's hard not to fall short. When we look in the mirror, we tell ourselves how wrong we are, how fat, how old, how ugly, compared to those models, that self-talk leads to lower self-esteem. And lower self-esteem leads to all sorts of problems.

Feelings *always* correspond to words and pictures. Our system works a little like a computer: the programs we respond to are the images and words we say to ourselves or are said to us. A part of our brain called the limbic system has the integrative function of having feelings match the stimulus provided it. Self-esteem is the sense/feeling we have about ourselves after a lifetime of messages we finally believe.

Very bright people feel stupid because they were told by others and now tell themselves that they are dumb. Beautiful and slender women feel fat because they compare themselves to size zero and tell themselves a million times how fat they are. Reality becomes imagination times vividness. The continual repetition either from the inner or outer world makes for vividness and causes our powerful feelings. If we want to change our feelings we *must* change the internal words and pictures we say to ourselves. It is not the events of our lives that dictate our feelings; it is our internal and external response to those events.

A Glaring Incongruity

There is a 90% to 95% level of recidivism in weight loss programs 2-5 years out and yet this is a $40 billion dollar industry a year. Why do rational people throw their money at something with such a miserable long-term track record and why does the industry content itself with this level of failure?

Reframing Loss

What do you do when you lose something? Most of us try and find it again.

What do you do when you throw something away? Most leave it thrown away and forget about it.

Now advertisers know the power of language and yet all the ads are to your conscious mind/self about how much you want to lose. Your conscious mind which has been programmed by the outside world decides what it wants to lose and sets that as a goal. Do you think anyone in the industry invites you to consult the unconscious mind, which, after all, is losing a part of itself? Not on your life.

Form Follows Function

All the contracts are made with the conscious mind. There is no realization that "holding weight" probably has an unconscious and *positive* purpose and therefore it is impossible to find an alternative way to accomplish this purpose. Weight then becomes the enemy, something to fight. Weight becomes the enemy, something to fight. The battle is on. The conscious mind loses the weight, the unconscious mind, not having been consulted or honored, goes to find what it has lost. And so the battle goes for years.

Some psychologists understand the dynamics of the ways we protect ourselves with weight, the many appetites we try to fill through food—our hunger for love, for intimacy, for passion, for self-expression. We know that many victims of molestation have insulated themselves from pain by adding layers of fat. Many have unconsciously made themselves heavy so that they will be unat-

172

tractive enough to avoid sexual assault. We have an ecological system. Every aspect of our bodies and minds has a function.

Why don't we get rid of the word *loss* altogether when it comes to weight and use language that reinforces the long-term outcome that we want? We need to address this issue in new ways.

- What are you willing to let go of?
- What do you no longer need to carry around?
- What other ways can you find to protect yourself?
- What else can you use to fill up your needs besides food?
- What are you ready to throw away?
- *What other ways can you nourish and fulfill yourself?*

There are numerous creative ways to approach the subject of getting rid of excess weight. Many advertisers use the long tested strategies that invite women to hate themselves and therefore get us to spend a fortune on products that promise us a better and happier life .

The Roots of the Problem

While our propensity for self-hatred is exacerbated by the media, the roots of it can be found in the messages we assimilated at a very early age from family, the culture at large and the media. When we are very young we begin to introject certain things, to incorporate ideas unconsciously into our psyche. We assimilate these ideas before we are able to decide whether we believe them or not.

As babies, we open our mouths and swallow everything we're fed. The same thing happens with attitudinal responses. We get programmed. We do what we see, we repeat what we hear, we mimic—all that is introjecting things. Metaphorically, we don't have the mental teeth to chew things up, think things through. We are too young to decide what is good for us or not, what fits, if we agree or not. We just take it in and it becomes synonymous with who we are.

90% of girls between 3 and 11 years have at least one Barbie doll, and many have more than one. For most of these girls, Barbie is their first standard of beauty. And what are her dimensions? 38-18-28.

One out of 100,000 women could achieve the statistics of Barbie if she had plastic surgery and removed several ribs. So one out of 100,000 leaves 99,999 of us feeling like we don't measure up to our earliest childhood symbol of beauty.

As parents we need to be vigilant about what we're exposing our children to. The vast majority of kids today are being brought up in households with two working parents. Television is usually a baby sitter. Parents don't give an appropriate message.

Self-esteem is an amalgam of what we hear and see in the outside world and what we hear and see in our inside world.

If a child is bombarded with messages from the media, these messages are going to have a profound influence over what she tells herself about who she is. If she doesn't look like Barbie, and Barbie is her measure of beauty, what does that do to her self-image?

Closing the Gap

The gap between reality and expectations is where disappointment and frustration and anger breed. The higher the expectations, and the further they are from reality, the more room there is for all those negative emotions. And when we have those negative emotions, we often deal with them by eating too much, buying too much, doing any number of things to excess. We try to do something so we don't have to feel so bad.

So it's very important to try to close the gap between our reality and expectations. We need to have expectations that fit our body type, our metabolism. We need *realistic* expectations for ourselves that support our health, self-love and self-acceptance.

Many of us are in some state of crisis now because we are acting out of self-hatred, out of fear and insecurity. Accumulated dis-ease in one's life sets up conditions for compromised immunity which can contribute to a climate for emotional and physical disease. Our emotional and physical health is greatly affected by how we feel about ourselves, and the steps we can take to improve our self-esteem are important steps in our journey toward high-level wellness.

In cybernetics there is a law called the *law of requisite variety*. That law says "any element, human or machine that has the widest range of variability will control." In simple terms, those of us with the greatest flexibility and the widest range of behavioral responses will be in more control of our lives. Lose/gain is a binary system and doesn't offer enough choices for most of us to succeed when it comes to weight and its associated effects. True choice is when we go beyond opposites and have many options to achieve our desired outcome. If long term weight reduction is our goal, then we are going to have to design strategies quite different from those of an industry that gets all of its money from our repeated failures.

It's time to wake up and rethink what is healthy for *ourselves*. Time to pay attention to what we're taking in and putting out so that we're conscious in the onslaught of manipulative ads, conscious of what we say to ourselves and others about who we are, knowing full well the power of our words.

For the life of us, it's time to redefine beauty in such a way that it is big enough to include ourselves and those we love. We need to define it in dimensions beyond the physical. It is this mindfulness, this courage that will ensure the body/mind/spirit health that we are all hungry for and all seeking.

Cathy

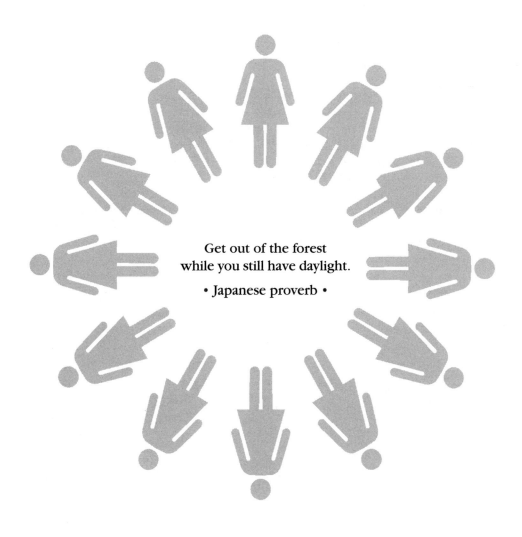

Get out of the forest
while you still have daylight.

• Japanese proverb •

A CALL TO ACTION

We hope that this book will serve as a springboard for more dialogue on the subject of body image and its impact on our physical, emotional, and spiritual well-being. The following sample exercises are meant to help you use this book as a way of exploring the relationship between health and self-image.

- As you read each woman's story, talk to yourself or another about the ways in which that story relates to you and your life. Have you had similar experiences or opposite ones? What is your version of what this woman is talking about? If you were called upon to give a response to this woman, what would you say to her?

- Get together with three or more women and form your own group. Each woman read a story and use that story as a springboard for discussions that are self revealing about your issues with your body in this culture. Have you had friends or family with similar issues?

- Start a journal and write your impressions and what each story means to you. Stay with one story a day and reflect as you move through that day on what ways you see or interface with others that may be a version of what you have read.

- As you move through your day, notice the particular type of ads you see that might contribute to the negative self-image of so many women in this country. Notice your self-talk about those ads. Make a conscious decision about what products to support based on how the ads invite you to feel about yourself.

- In your small women's group, brainstorm ways that you can make a difference in combating the narrow and exclusive definitions of beauty in this culture. It can be as simple as changing your internal talk. It could be complaining to store managers if they don't have choices of clothes in your size. It could be reading books on positive images to teach our young girls.

- Write your own story about what it has been for you growing up in a beauty and thin-obsessed culture. Think about ways you could start to do some of your own healing. Write down the activities that would lead to that and make a commitment to action for the plan you come up with.

- Name all the aspects of yourself that you value apart from the physical, such as intellectual, spiritual, emotional, etc. Each day write down three non-physical aspects of yourself that you value. Put them in a box. When feeling down, take a handful of those statements and give yourself a heaping plateful of positive reinforcement.

178

- Use some of the following questions for small group discussion:
  - How do you define beauty?
  - Is your definition of beauty wide enough to include yourself?
  - What are the most common internal messages you say to yourself about your body? Where did they come from?
  - If you could change something about your body, would you? What would you change? How do you think this would impact your life?
  - How do you feel when a woman much smaller than you starts talking about how fat she is?
  - Who in your life has made you feel the most beautiful? How?

- We frequently tell ourselves we can or can't have certain foods. It is as if we break down our world into absolute "Yeses" and "Nos." In fact, life is a series of priorities and choices.

  List 5 or 10 foods you love and usually place in the "No" or "I can't have that" category. Then, identify 5 important priorities for you, such as "I want to feel good in my clothes," or "I want to be at a weight that supports health," etc. Write these 5 priorities on an index card and keep it with you at all times. When food choice comes up, take out your index card and review your priorities.

179

Women's girdles are a driving safety hazard.
A well-encased woman driver tends to squirm,
which takes her attention away from her driving,
and fights back against the garter pull,
pushing down with her accelerator foot.

• *Canadian Survey* •

There is no foundation for these statements.

• *Girdle Manufacturers* •

THE THREE OF US

When I look to what fuels me for the journey, what helps me through the dark, I see that at every threshold, it is the women in my life who hold the light. And how they help is not by saying "go here, go there," but by sharing with me their own journeys through the rough terrain.

Thirty years ago when I left the convent and tried to find a new way in the world, every path I took seemed wrong. I was too much the renegade to fit in my community, and too much the nun to feel at home in my culture. In my early twenties, I had little self-awareness, less self-esteem, and was enraged and devastated by this rejection from my superiors.

In my mid-twenties, the second wave of feminism crashed upon my shore. When I sat in my first women's circle, listening to the stories of our lives, I was stunned by the similarities that surfaced. We had assimilated all the same lessons—to look and act a certain way, to follow men's lead, to defer to authority, to be docile and polite and hospitable. We all knew exactly what we were *supposed* to be doing, but struggled to uncover what we *wanted* to be doing, or more precisely, what we wanted to *be*.

We circled and talked for months and months, each of us revealing our deepest fears, our long-held secrets, our anger and disenchantment and visions of a life that we ourselves ordained. And what happened in that circle was that we *spoke ourselves into being*. Through the sharing of our stories, we discovered who we were, what we wanted, what was and was not acceptable. We healed ourselves, fortified ourselves. And when the doors opened, we emerged en masse as strong women, brave women, women tuned in to our own desire, in touch with and informed by our own wisdom.

Over the years, I have done what I could to encourage this life-giving process of sharing our stories. In the 80s I traveled around the world as a peace activist/photographer creating an occasion for people to gather and share our visions of a peaceful world. With fellow activists, I helped birth the Syracuse Cultural Workers to create an opening and clearinghouse for life-affirming art. I marched in countless human rights demonstrations for all of us who are marginalized and vilified for causes beyond our control.

In the 90s, my attention took a turn inward, calling me into my deeper places, so I could ponder and write of the world I envision and am co-creating. From this calm place came the confidence to teach, to hold a mirror to others' potential, encouraging my sisters and brothers to speak their truths.

And I see this book as another mirror, a compilation of stories that may reveal us to ourselves, unravel some of our mysteries, unleash some of our courage. This is the power, the alchemy of truth-telling—that one's sorrow, when spoken, can source another's strength; one's fear, when shared, can move another to action.

In a bookstore today, I came across a quote by Filipina activist, Dazzle Rivera: "As activists, we must adopt a mind-set of anticipation. We must no longer surf the wave. We must become the wind that creates the wave."

The voices in these stories are the vortex of just such a wind.

I come to this project as a change agent.

Long before I became a change agent I came to this world as a person who never quite fit what the world wanted me to be. I never understood why there was a way I was supposed to be—and I understood even less why I was nowhere near what those expectations were. Formal education never made sense to me; its presentation bored me. I wanted to be doing things and trying out ideas, not reading about them and regurgitating what I read.

I went to small private schools but fit into none. The first six years of school I went to a predominantly boys school. I was one of two girls in the class. I didn't fit but learned to do the activities of sports and shop that boys did. At age eleven, I woke up one day and was five feet eleven inches tall. My body had betrayed me; my childhood was lost. I looked like a grown woman and was responded to as such. From seventh grade to grade twelve, I went to a private girls school and again, I didn't fit. I was always ten going on 40 and spent most my time with people far older than I. There, I felt at home.

I went to a huge university and felt isolated in my freshman class of over ten thousand. I related more to my teachers than my classmates. I didn't fit. The oddity of it all was that inside, I did fit. I knew who I was, I knew what I responded to, I knew what I believed in, I knew who I loved, I knew what made sense to me. I felt strong and centered, as well as small and vulnerable. I was extraordinarily intuitive, seeing and knowing things that most people didn't. I thought everybody noticed inner feelings and internal conflicts. I said things I thought people knew. They didn't. I scared them, and again, I didn't fit.

In the sixties, I was a passionate protester believing for sure that my friends and I could make a difference, change the world, end the war. I was devastated that neither happened. Instead, I ended up clinically depressed and, once again, didn't fit. I learned to pretend and appear as if I fit. Few, if any, knew of my inner turmoil. I was tired of school and I wanted to go to work and do things.

After completing my undergraduate degree, I ran a center for criminally abused and neglected kids. They didn't fit and I knew how to reach them. I could make a difference in their lives. In that role, I fit. I later went back to graduate school, the formal walls of the kind of education I hated but it was okay then because I knew what ticket I needed to be able to go out and make a world that made sense to me.

With my masters in hand, I entered the world of traditional psychiatric hospitals. My work with the patients made perfect sense, but my interface with the medical system made no sense—even 25 years ago. I tried for five years to make the way psychiatry was practiced make sense. It never did. A lot of my creativity got channeled into anger trying to change a system that had a huge stake in the status quo. I didn't want to be that angry. They all thought they were doing good medicine. I didn't fit. I went to the mountains for a month. It became clear to me that I had to leave the whole "comfortable" world that looked like it fit for me and find another way to live, to work, to love or I would die. At 29, I "dropped out" of the world for a year, left the man I shared my life with, the job which had defined me, and gave myself as much time as my life savings would give me to find a way to fit.

It was the hardest and best year of my life. At the end of that year, I found home within myself and the courage to make a life where I did fit. I left the east coast and came west. I was never again employed by another. I did work that made sense to me. It was clear, outcome-oriented work with clients—private and corporate. I let the marketplace decide whether I was good enough to be employed. If I had a full private practice and satisfied corporate clients, I was satisfied that my work was effective. I had no one to tell me my work was good or bad. Clients came wanting some sort of help to profoundly change their life. I was a good guide, they were courageous travelers. Their lives changed and I had the privilege of being a part of their journey.

If I look at how mainstream America lives, loves and works, I suppose I don't fit. The difference is, I don't want to fit into that mold. I want to live with integrity, accountability, intensity, consciousness, curiosity, creativity, and mostly with reality. Consciousness has become a counter culture activity. I am happily counter culture. What makes me powerful as a guide and a change agent is not what I learned in school, it is what I learned in life: being me in a world that invited me as a woman to be everybody but me. I am willing to share that life and journey with others, to give them the courage to know that they can create any world that they have the willingness and courage to try. As a change agent, I want to challenge people to go beyond the barriers of what they see as their limitations. I believe that as we own who and what we are, we start to own our own real personal power to create a world that works and fits our own unique energy. As a woman and as a psychotherapist, that is my work and that is my life. Work and life have become seamless for me.

I still am far from the norm in every way that my culture has set for me. Everybody I see in the world also doesn't fit into the "cookie cutter" mold, physically, emotionally, intellectually or spiritually.

These stories and the pain they reveal are a call to arms. In sharing them, we ask other women to join these courageous women. Share your stories, your pain, your survival strategies. Use these as the springboard to form new emotional clothes. We all deserve to fit. Make your own pattern and try it on. I did and I came to love me for who I am, not for how I don't fit.

I am a lover
— a lover who learned how to fight.

I never had to fight my parents, wondering at times if I missed something—or passed on some wonderful neuroses, having to acknowledge mine with no one to blame. Thank you Charles and Renée Meynet.

I never had to fight my siblings — although at times, as a kid, I sure tried. Thank you Claude and Roland, and thank you, Alain —sitting on your cloud, I presume, looking at us, still cracking a joke with your inimitable wit.

I fought as a student, deciding to become an architect in spite of countless road blocks. I crossed the finish-line. I won.

I fought as an architect, establishing myself in a profession dominated by men. I won.

I fought as a person, electing to move away from the cocoon of a loving family to embrace another country, another culture, another language. I made them mine. I won.

I fought as a mother, relinquishing my rights when giving my son up for adoption. I lost twenty-eight precious years of nurturing and love—as well as anguish and aggravations. I won when Bill returned, twenty-eight years later, bright, loving, caring, giving, a testimonial to his parents who gave him what I didn't have to give. Thank you Bill. Thank you Ron and Bev Attinger.

I never had to fight as a wife, sharing a thirty-two year partnership based on love, trust, respect, shared goals and laughter. Thank you Russell.

I fought as a stepmother, striving to embrace, to understand, to accept. I won in so many ways—each one precious to me—I can't count. I am a winner. Thank you Lynn.

A clique of longtime loyal friends form the backbone of my support system. All these years, never a fight. I cherish your loyal friendship more than words can express.

When I made the decision to expand my horizons beyond architecture, I fought business conventions and ready-made labels. Applying analytical skills in uncharted venues, selling my way of addressing challenges, resolving problems and finding effective business and marketing solutions, I became a "Catalyst." Giving my all, never feeling that it is enough, and always striving for "more better," I gained an enviable, loyal clientele. Thank you, each one of you, for your trust. You make me a winner.

Lastly, I fought my two project partners about the book structure and its symbolic cover. We all won. We won through the understanding and respect we developed for our differences and our similarities:

Jan, loving and caring, felt the public joys and the private pains of each individual in the circle of women. The sensitive photojournalist she is saw the book as a documentary on a common cry for help.

Cathy, dedicated mental health care practitioner—a practical practitioner—approached the circle of women clinically, caringly. Addressing the issue logically, she was a crucial pivot between the unit and the whole.

I am a fighter
— a fighter who knows how to love.

I wanted to use the women's pain to shout the urgency of the issue. I didn't want to soothe; I wanted to lay the wound wide open for everyone to see and, through its disquieting, haunting message, question our passive submission to indoctrinations that preclude us from retaining and celebrating our individuality, in all forms and shapes.

We fought until we recognized that we were a microcosm of the women we honor in these pages. We became a tripod, our bearings in different backgrounds and cultures, reaching for a common goal.

I won.
I won two friends.
Thank you Cathy and Jan

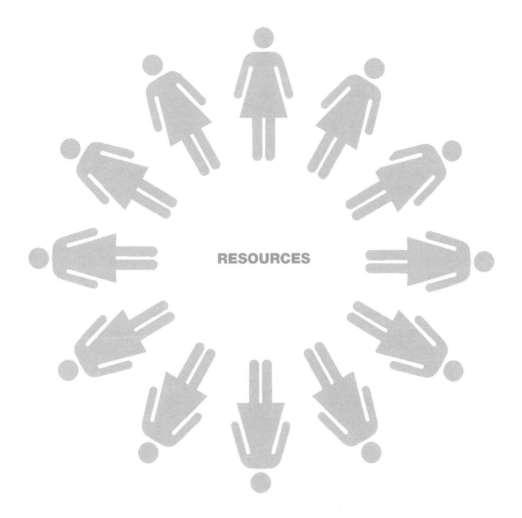

RESOURCES

When I was young, my producer, George Tyler, told me that were I four inches taller I could become one of the greatest actresses of my time. I decided to lick my size. A string of teachers pulled and stretched till I felt I was in a medieval torture chamber. I gained nary an inch—but my posture became military. I became the tallest five-foot woman in the world. And my refusal to be limited by my limitations enabled me to play Mary of Scotland, one of the tallest queens in history.

• Helen Hayes •

The books and websites listed here are a small sampling of what is available in print and on the web; each one includes extensive bibliographies and links to related topics.

Bibliography:

Apostolides, Maryann. *Inner Hunger: A Young Woman's Struggle Through Anorexia and Bulimia*. New York: W.W. Norton and Company, Inc., 1998.

Bauermeister, Erica and Smith, Holly. *Let's Hear It For Girls: 375 Great Books for Readers 2-14*. New York: Viking Penguin, 1999.

Bordo, Susan. *Unbearable Weight: Feminism, Western Culture and the Body*. Berkeley: University of California Press, 1995.

Brumberg, Joan Jacobs. *The Body Project: An Intimate History of American Girls*. New York: Vintage Books, 1998.

Edut, Ophira, ed. *Adios, Barbie: Young Women Write about Body Image and Identity*. Seattle: Seal Press, 1998.

Fallon, Patricia, Katzman, Melanie A., Wooley, Susan C., eds. *Feminist Perspectives on Eating Disorders*. New York: Guilford Publications, Inc., 1996.

Gray, Heather, and Phillips, Samantha. *Real Girl/Real World: Tools for Finding Your True Self*. Seattle: Seal Press, 1998.

Haiken, Elizabeth. *Venus Envy: A History of Cosmetic Surgery*. Baltimore: Johns Hopkins University Press, 1997.

Hales, Dianne. *Just Like a Woman: How Gender Science is Revealing What Makes Us Female*. New York: Bantam Books, 1999.

Halprin, Sara. *Look at My Ugly Face: Myths and Musings on Beauty and Other Perilous Obsessions with Women's Appearance*. New York: Viking Penguin, 1996.

Odean, Kathleen. *Great Books for Girls: More Than 600 Books to Inspire Today's Girls and Tomorrow's Women*. New York: Ballantine Books, 1997.

Peiss, Kathy. *Hope in a Jar: The Making of America's Beauty Culture*. New York: Henry Holt and Company, LLC, 1999.

Shaevitz, Marjorie Hansen. *The Confident Woman: Learn the Rules of the Game.* New York: Crown Publishing Group, Inc., 1999.

Wolfe, Naomi. *The Beauty Myth: How Images of Beauty are Used Against Women*. New York: Doubleday, 1992.

Websites:

www.realwomenproject.com
The Real Women Project is a multi-sensory exploration of body image and its profound impact on women's health and well being.

www.about-face.org
About-Face is a media literacy organization focused on the impact mass media has on the physical, mental and emotional well being of women and girls.

www.bodypositive.com
Looks at ways we can feel good in the bodies we have.
"Remember, your body hears everything you think."

www.iVillage.com
Real solutions for real women

www.oxygen.com
The first online and on-air network for women, by women.

www.electrapages.com
A directory of women's organizations

www.women.com
The Smart Way to Get Things Done

www.goaskalice.columbia.edu (Columbia U. Health Service)
Offers younger women an opportunity to "go ask Alice" about physical, emotional, and spiritual health issues

www.something-fishy.com
An eating disorders website

www.allhealth.com
Features information on recent medical research

www.4women.gov (U.S. Public Health Service),
Links to scores of federal agencies and publications, as well as to private sector organizations concerned with women's health issues

www.mayohealth.org
Click on Mayo Clinics Women's BodyPositive Center for news of medical break-throughs and referrals to comprehensive collections of articles covering all health issues

www.gurze.com
An eating disorders resource site

www.healthjourneys.com
Introduces people to the healing powers of the mind through the use of guided imagery. It features the best tape on weight issues.

www.onhealth.com/ch1/resource/conditions/sub7.asp
Sign up for monthly e-mail reminders to examine your breasts.

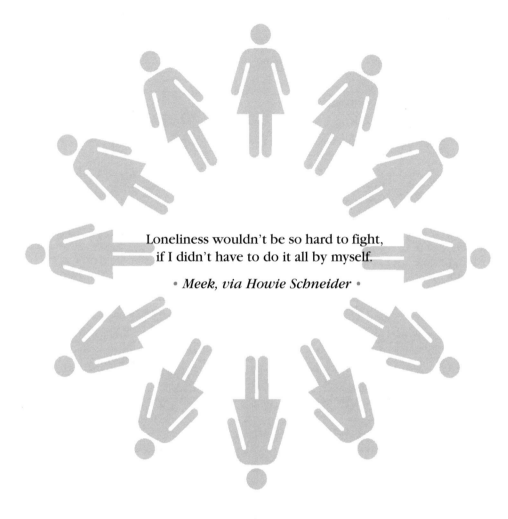

Loneliness wouldn't be so hard to fight,
if I didn't have to do it all by myself.

• *Meek, via Howie Schneider* •

STORY INDEX

STORY INDEX

ORDER FORMS
for

A WAIST IS A TERRIBLE THING TO MIND
by Jan Phillips, Cathy Conheim, LCSW, and Christine Forester

AND OTHER BOOKS BY THE SAME AUTHORS

ORDER FORM   **A WAIST IS A TERRIBLE THING TO MIND**
by Jan Phillips, Cathy Conheim, LCSW, and Christine Forester

Name _____ Telephone: _____

Company Name _____ e-mail: _____

Address _____

City _____ State + Zip _____

Please send _____ copies @ $16.95 .... $ _____ $ _____
20% discount on purchase of 5 or more copies .... $ _____
Subtotal .... $ _____
7.75% California sales tx (when applicable) .... $ _____
Packing and shipping @ $3.50 per book • $2.50 each additional copy .... $ _____

Total amount payable to Breakthrough Press .... $ _____

Prepayment required with each order unless otherwise agreed upon with the publisher.
Please send check to: Breakthrough Press • Box 135 • La Jolla • CA 92038   www.breakthroughpress.com

---

ORDER FORM   **A WAIST IS A TERRIBLE THING TO MIND**
by Jan Phillips, Cathy Conheim, LCSW, and Christine Forester

Name _____ Telephone: _____

Company Name _____ e-mail: _____

Address _____

City _____ State + Zip _____

Please send _____ copies @ $16.95 .... $ _____ $ _____
20% discount on purchase of 5 or more copies .... $ _____
Subtotal .... $ _____
7.75% California sales tx (when applicable) .... $ _____
Packing and shipping @ $3.50 per book • $2.50 each additional copy .... $ _____

Total amount payable to Breakthrough Press .... $ _____

Prepayment required with each order unless otherwise agreed upon with the publisher.
Please send check to: Breakthrough Press • Box 135 • La Jolla • CA 92038   www.breakthroughpress.com

---

ORDER FORM   **A WAIST IS A TERRIBLE THING TO MIND**
by Jan Phillips, Cathy Conheim, LCSW, and Christine Forester

Name _____ Telephone: _____

Company Name _____ e-mail: _____

Address _____

City _____ State + Zip _____

Please send _____ copies @ $16.95 .... $ _____ $ _____
20% discount on purchase of 5 or more copies .... $ _____
Subtotal .... $ _____
7.75% California sales tx (when applicable) .... $ _____
Packing and shipping @ $3.50 per book • $2.50 each additional copy .... $ _____

Total amount payable to Breakthrough Press .... $ _____

Prepayment required with each order unless otherwise agreed upon with the publisher
Please send check to: Breakthrough Press • Box 135 • La Jolla • CA 92038   www.breakthroughpress.com

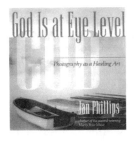

God Is at Eye Level—Photography as a Healing Art • Quest Books (May 2000) • $21.95

This is a book about photography's power to heal, transform, bridge gaps between people when language falls short. Photography is embraced as a practice that can lead to flashes of surprising insight and open doors to a deeper knowing. "May we, as image makers, shapers of the culture, set our sights on things we value, rituals we engage in that heal and serve. May our images honor the ordinary endeavors of common people, and may they make their way to the eyes of the weary—light to the dark, fire to the chill." • from *God Is at Eye Level*

"Jan's wealth of talent, fearless voice, and fomenting creativity have resulted in a wondrous book that is part photographic exhibit, part memoir, part spiritual teaching, and part self-help workshop. Each luminous element could stand proudly on its own, but we get all four. What can I say? Buy, view, read, and love this book!"

Belleruth Naparstek • *author of* Your Sixth Sense

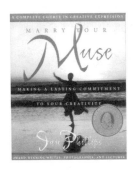

Marry Your Muse—Making a Lasting Commitment to Your Creativity • Quest Books (1998) • $18.

Winner of the 1998 Ben Franklin Award, this book offers a complete course in creative expression. Anyone who wants to experience life as a work of art will find inspiration and practical suggestions in this joyous book. It includes poignant and provocative essays, insightful exercises, and dozens of compelling photographs. "Do not doubt that you were born to create. Do not believe for a minute that the realm of art belongs only to others…Find what brings you joy and go there. That is your place to create, to move with the spirit, for the Muse lingers near the home of our joy." • from *Marry Your Muse*

"Marry Your Muse is an affirmation that a life lived creatively is not only a possibility, but a promise and a practice available to all of us."

Michael Jones • *composer of* Pianoscapes

Making Peace: One Woman's Journey Around the World
(Friendship Press, 1989) $18.95

Making Peace is a book of photographs and reflections
about an 18 month global peace pilgrimage. It is an account of the author's spiritual transformation as she
moved from her Western, Christian, social activist roots
into cultures and communities that challenged her values at every juncture. "In order to create a culture of peace,
a culture that reflects our reverence for life, we need stories and symbols that heal and guide, that help us remember we are part of a whole." • from *Making Peace*

"This is a splendid book! A vivid account of one daring, inquisitive woman's
search for the things that make for peace."

• Carter Heyward •
author, Touching Our Strength

These books are available from www.amazon.com; Quest Books (800-669-9425);
Friendship Press (513- 948-8733). Signed copies may be purchased from Jan
Phillips. She may be contacted at 858-571-1417 or at www.janphillips.com.

Jan Phillips presents workshops and keynote addresses nationally.

ALSO WRITTEN BY CHRISTINE FORESTER

Let's Face It… The Decision is Mine !
Press-on-Press • $6.95

A farcical little book. Forty-seven witty, yet thought-provoking, illustrated alternatives as to what anyone and everyone can do with their lives.

"Funny"…"Philosophical"…"The perfect gift if you want to send someone a reason to smile."

Digby Diehl
Book Editor & Literary Critic
"Good Morning, America"

"The more you read
Marie-Christine Forester,
the more you'll want to read
more and much more-ester."

Ted Geisel (Dr. Seuss)
Pulitzer Prizewinner

"I am going to use *Let's Face It !* as a little shaper-upper for someone who needs a little loving spank…"

Marion Ross
Actress
(Mrs. Cunningham, Happy Days TV series)

"Along with Peale and Pogg, add Forester at the of the list of entertaining positive thinkers."

Pete Wilson
former U.S. Senator
former California Governor

"*Let's Face It !* deserves a place on anyone's coffee table, whether at the office or in the home !"

Marjorie Hansen Shaevitz
Author, The Confident Woman

"*Let's Face It !* Christine Forester's book is wonderfull."

Spencer Johnson, MD
Author,
Co-author, The One Minute Manager

"Left brained message written by a right brained pen."

Natasha Josefowitz
Author/Lecturer

… "you'll love *Let's Face It !*"

Neil Morgan
Associate Editor, Senior Columnist
San Diego Union-Tribune

Let's Face It ! is available for $6.95 (+ 3.25 postage & handling) from:
Press-on-Press • Box 135 • La Jolla • California 92038 • forester@san.rr.com

The body is a sacred garment.
It is your first and last garment.
It is what you enter life in,
and what you depart with,
and it should be treated
with honor.

• Martha Graham •